Data Access in the ASP.NET 2.0 Framework

Stephen Walther

800 East 96th Street, Indianapolis, Indiana 46240 USA

Data Access in the ASP.NET 2.0 Framework (Video LiveLessons)

For information regarding permissions, write to:

Pearson Education, Inc
Rights and Contracts Department
501 Boylston Street, Suite 900
Boston, MA 02116
Fax (617) 671 3447

Library of Congress Cataloging-in-Publication Data:

Walther, Stephen.
 Data access in the ASP.NET 2.0 framework (video livelessons) / Stephen Walther.
    p. cm.
 ISBN 0-672-32952-2
 1. Active server pages. 2. Web sites—Design. 3. Web site development. 4. Microsoft .NET. I. Title.
TK5105.8885.A26W356 2007
005.2'76—dc22

                                                                    2007029188

Visit us on the Web: www.samspublishing.com

Corporate and Government Sales

The publisher offers excellent discounts on this book when ordered in quantity for bulk purchases or special sales, which may include electronic versions and/or custom covers and content particular to your business, training goals, marketing focus, and branding interests. For more information, please contact:

U.S. Corporate and Government Sales
(800) 382-3419
corpsales@pearsontechgroup.com

For sales outside the United States please contact:

International Sales
international@pearsoned.com

Warning and Disclaimer

This book and video product is designed to provide information about data access in the ASP.NET 2.0 framework. Every effort has been made to make this book as complete and as accurate as possible, but no warranty or fitness is implied.

The information provided is on an "as is" basis. The author and the publisher shall have neither liability nor responsibility to any person or entity with respect to any loss or damages arising from the information contained in this book or from the use of the DVD or programs accompanying it.

The opinions expressed in this LiveLesson belong to the author and are not necessarily those of Sams Publishing.

ISBN-13: 978-0-672-32952-4
ISBN-10: 0-672-32952-2

Text printed in the United States at RR Donnelley in Crawfordsville, Indiana.
First printing, September 2007

Editor-in-Chief
Karen Gettman

Acquisitions Editor
Neil Rowe

Managing Editor
Gina Kanouse

Senior Project Editor
Kristy Hart

Copy Editor
Jovana San Nicolas-Shirley
Water Crest Publishing

Proofreader
Mike Henry

Publishing Coordinator
Cindy Teeters

Multimedia Developer
Eric Strom

Designer
Gary Adair

Composition
Nonie Ratcliff

Feedback Information

At Pearson, our goal is to create in-depth technical books of the highest quality and value. Each product is crafted with care and precision, undergoing rigorous development that involves the unique expertise of members from the professional technical community.

Readers' feedback is a natural continuation of this process. If you have any comments regarding how we could improve the quality of this book, or otherwise alter it to better suit your needs, you can contact us through e-mail at mylivelessons@pearsoned.com. Please make sure to include the title and ISBN in your message.

We greatly appreciate your assistance.

Trademark Acknowledgments

All terms mentioned in this book that are known to be trademarks or service marks have been appropriately capitalized. Neither Sams Publishing nor Pearson Education, Inc., can attest to the accuracy of this information. Use of a term in this book should not be regarded as affecting the validity of any trademark or service mark.

Table of Contents

Workbook Introduction

This workbook is divided into three sections. The first section contains a step-by-step companion to the video. Each of the modules in the video is written out into steps to make it easier to review the steps after you watch the video.

The second section of this workbook contains an introduction to SQL, the language of databases. If you are new to Microsoft SQL Server 2005, or entirely new to the SQL language, you should review this section of the workbook before viewing the video. The video assumes that you are familiar with the SQL language. If not, no worries—read the SQL introduction in the section later in the workbook.

Finally, the third section of this workbook contains an introduction to the ASP.NET 2.0 framework. Again, the video assumes that you are familiar with the basics of the ASP.NET framework. If you are completely new to the ASP.NET framework, you should definitely read this section of the workbook before watching the video.

NOTE

If you are interested in reading a comprehensive book on the ASP.NET 2.0 Framework, permit me to recommend my book *ASP.NET 2.0 Unleashed*. This book covers every aspect of the ASP.NET 2.0 framework.

---

module ⊙ 1

Getting Familiar with the Visual Studio 2005 Development Environment

Microsoft Visual Studio 2005 is the most popular development environment for building ASP.NET 2.0 applications. Visual Studio 2005 is available in several different editions:

- Visual Studio Express Edition (Visual Web Developer)

- Visual Studio Standard Edition

- Visual Studio Professional Edition

- Visual Studio Team System

For a detailed comparison of the different editions, see http://msdn.microsoft.com/vstudio/products/compare.

To follow along with the programming samples in this video, you need to have one of the Visual Studio 2005 editions installed on your machine. If you don't own Visual Studio 2005, you can download Visual Studio Express (more commonly known as Visual Web Developer) from http://msdn.microsoft.com/vstudio/express/vwd.

Creating a New Website

You create a new website by selecting the menu option **File**, **New Web Site** (see Figure 1). When you create a new website, you specify the location and language for the new website. Typically, you want to create a File System website using the Visual Basic programming language.

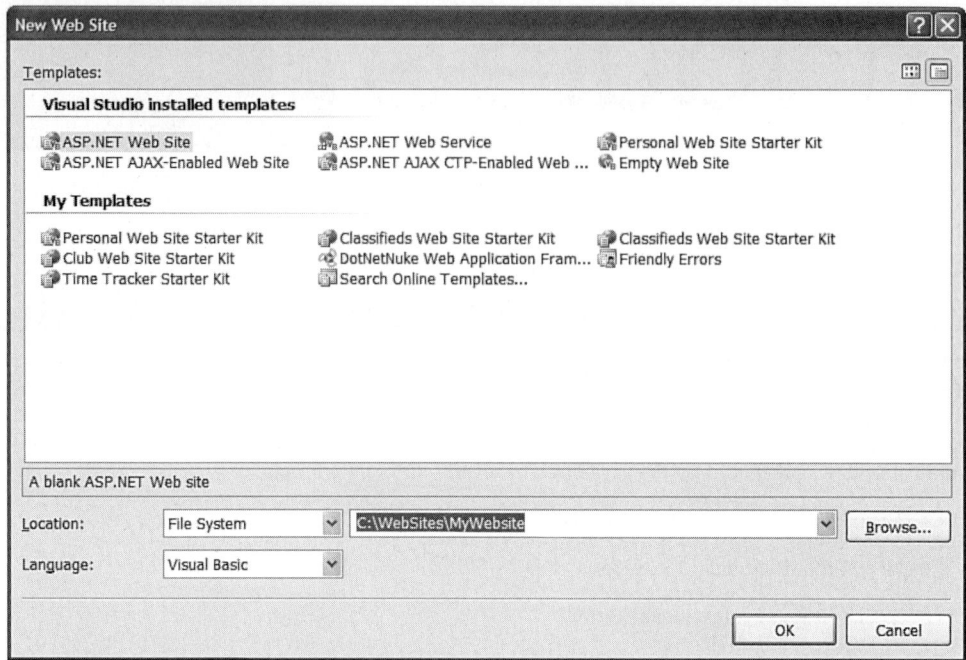

Figure 1   Creating a new website.

Using the Solution Explorer Window

The Solution Explorer window contains all the files for your project. You use the Solution Explorer window to pick files to edit. If the Solution Explorer window is not open, you can open it by selecting the menu option **View**, **Solution Explorer** (see Figure 2).

Figure 2   Using the Solution Explorer window.

Using the Editor Window

When you double-click an ASP.NET page in the Solution Explorer window, the page opens in the Editor window. Two views are available for an ASP.NET page: Design view and Source view. In Design view, you see how your page appears when the page is viewed in a browser. In Source view, you see the source code for your page. You can edit your page in either mode. To switch between the two views, you click the **Design** or **Source** tab located at the bottom left of the Editor window (see Figure 3).

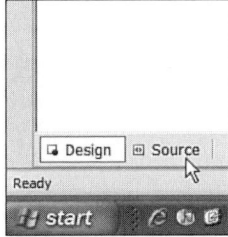

Figure 3   Switching between Design and Source view.

Using the Toolbox Window

The Toolbox window contains the ASP.NET controls and HTML elements that you can add to an ASP.NET page (see Figure 4). You can drag and drop items from the Toolbox window onto a page in either Source or Design view. The Toolbox window groups its items under different tabs. For example, the Data tab contains all the ASP.NET controls related to data access.

Figure 4   Expanding the Data tab in the Toolbox window.

Using the Properties Window

The Properties window enables you to view and modify ASP.NET control properties (see Figure 5). If the Properties window is not open, you can open this window by selecting the menu option **View**, **Properties window**. Alternatively, you can open the Properties window by right-clicking any ASP.NET control in the Editor and selecting the menu option **Properties**.

By default, properties are grouped by category. If you prefer, you can arrange the properties in alphabetical order by clicking the icon with the tooltip labeled alphabetical, which appears toward the top of the Properties window.

Figure 5   Viewing the properties for the GridView control.

Taking Advantage of Auto Hide

You can use a Visual Studio 2005 feature named Auto Hide to open and close windows automatically when you hover your mouse over a window. You enable Auto Hide for a window by clicking the pushpin that appears on a window's control menu (see Figure 6). You also have the option of enabling Auto Hide for all windows by selecting the menu option **Window**, **Auto Hide All**.

Figure 6   Enabling Auto Hide for the Solution Explorer window.

Running an ASP.NET Page

There are two ways you can run an ASP.NET page. First, you can right-click any page (in either the Editor or Solution Explorer window) and select **View in Browser**. When you use this option to view a page, the page is not opened in a debugger.

Alternatively, you can run an entire ASP.NET application. You run an entire application by selecting either the menu option **Debug**, **Start Debugging** or the menu option **Debug**, **Start without Debugging**. Before selecting either option, you should set a Start Page by right-clicking a page in the Solution Explorer window and selecting the menu option **Set As Start Page**.

When you run an application using the debugger, you can set breakpoints in your application code. Double-click to the left of the code where you want to set a breakpoint and a red-filled circle appears. When the line of code associated with the breakpoint executes, your application stops. You can hover your mouse over any variable in scope to see its current value (see Figure 7). You can step through your code line-by-line by selecting the menu option **Debug**, **Step Into** (or pressing the F11 key).

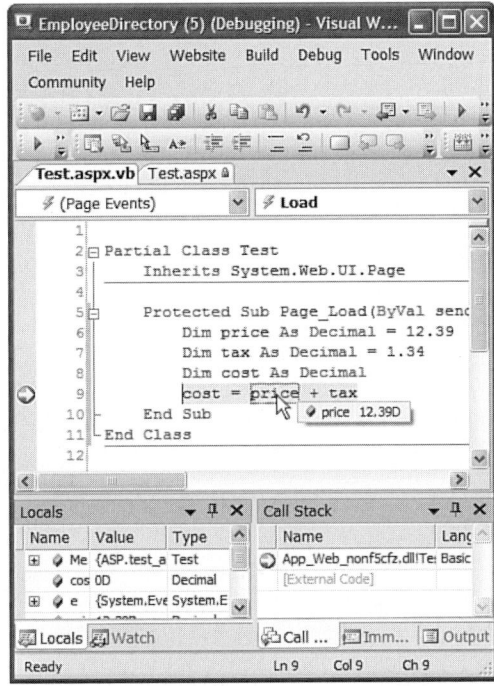

Figure 7   Hitting a breakpoint and viewing variable values.

module ⊙ 2

Creating an Employee Directory Application

The Employee Directory application illustrates how easily you can create a fully functional database-driven application in ASP.NET. This application enables you to display a list of employees, add new employees, and modify existing employee information. The amazing thing about this application is it is written with only two lines of code.

Creating the Employee Database Table

All the employee information is stored in a Microsoft SQL Server 2005 Express database. SQL Server Express is included with both Visual Studio 2005 and Visual Web Developer.

You create a new database by selecting the menu option **Website**, **Add New Item** and selecting the SQL Database item (see Figure 8). You are prompted to add the database to the App_Data folder.

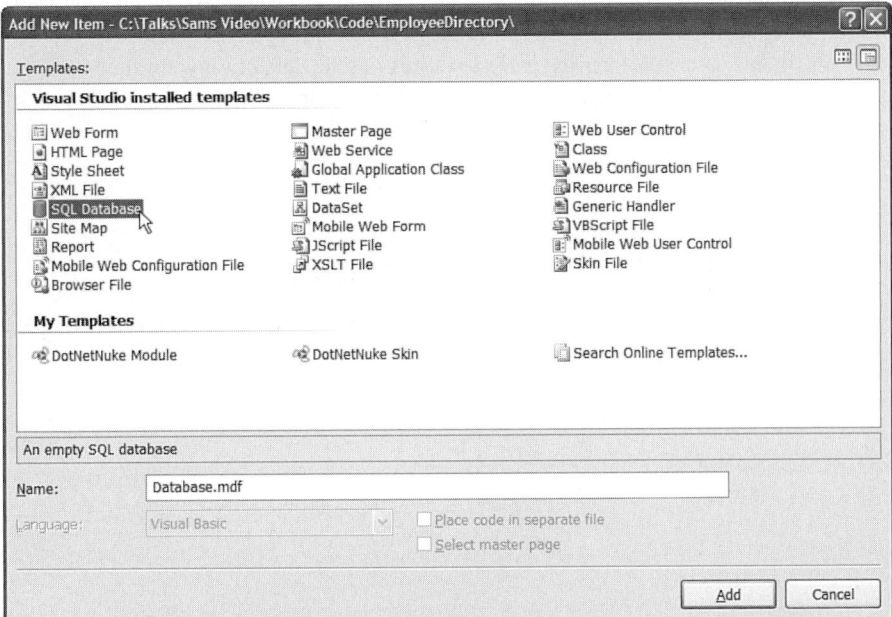

Figure 8   Creating a new SQL Server Express database.

After you create a new database, you can add database tables to the database by right-clicking the Tables folder in the Database Explorer window (named Server Explorer in Visual Studio 2005) and selecting **Add New Table**.

For the Employee Directory application, you need to create a database table with the following columns:

Column Name	Data Type	Allow Nulls
Id	int	false
LastName	nvarchar(150)	false
FirstName	nvarchar(150)	false
PhoneExtension	nvarchar(50)	false
Email	nvarchar(300)	false
DateCreated	datetime	false

Both the Id column and the DateCreated column have special properties. The Id column should be marked as a primary key column. You can mark the Id column as a primary key column by clicking the icon of the key, which appears toward the top of the Editor window.

Furthermore, the Id column must be an identity column. You can mark the Id column as an identity column by expanding Identity Specification under Column Properties and setting the property Is Identity to the value **Yes**. An identity column automatically generates a unique number for each row added to a table.

The DateCreated column needs to be provided with a default value. You assign a default value to a column by entering a value for the Default Value or Binding property in the list of Column Properties. In this case, you enter the value **GetDate()** as the default value for the DateCreated column. The GetDate() function returns the current date and time. By assigning this function as the default value of the DateCreated column, each row added to the database table gets a date and time stamp automatically.

Creating the Default.aspx Page

The Default.aspx page displays a list of all the employees contained in the Employee database table (see Figure 9). Follow these steps to create the Default.aspx page.

Figure 9   Displaying a list of company employees.

First, add the GridView control to the page:

1. Open the Default.aspx page in the Editor window by double-clicking the page in the Solution Explorer window.

2. Switch the Default.aspx page into Design view by clicking the **Design** tab, which appears at the bottom left of the Editor window.

3. Add a GridView control to the Default.aspx page by dragging the control from beneath the Data tab in the Toolbox window onto the page.

Next, configure the data source for the GridView:

4. Open the GridView Tasks window by clicking the **Smart Tasks** icon, which appears at the top-right corner of the GridView control (or right-click the GridView control and select the menu option **Show Smart Tag**).

5. Open the Data Source Configuration Wizard by selecting the **<New data source>** option from `Choose Data Source` in the GridView Tasks window.

6. When prompted to `Choose a Data Source Type`, select **Database**. Click the **OK** button.

7. When prompted to `Choose Your Data Connection`, click the **New Connection** button, select **Microsoft SQL Server Database File**, and browse to the EmployeesDB.mdf database file. Click the **Next** button.

8. When prompted to `Save the connection string to the application configuration file`, select **Yes**, and save the connection string with the name **EmployeesDBConnectionString**. Click the **Next** button.

9. When prompted to **Configure the Select Statement**, choose **Specify columns from a table or view**. For **Name**, select **Employees** and for **Columns**, select the **LastName, FirstName, and Email** columns. Click the **Next** button.

10. When prompted to **Test Query**, click the **Finish** button.

Finally, format the GridView control by completing these steps:

11. Select the **GridView** in the Editor window and open the **GridView** Tasks window.

12. Click the **Auto Format... task** to open the Auto Format dialog box.

13. Select a format scheme (such as my favorite, the Professional scheme) and click the **OK** button.

Creating the Add.aspx Page

The Add.aspx Web Form page enables you to add a new employee to the Employee Directory (see Figure 10). Follow these steps to create the Add.aspx page.

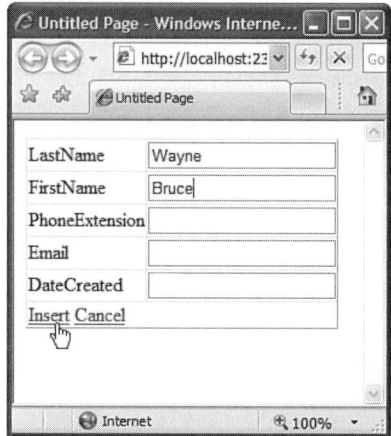

Figure 10   Adding a new employee to the Employee Directory.

First, create the Add.aspx page and link from the Default.aspx page to the Add.aspx page:

1. Create the Add.aspx page by selecting the menu option **Website, Add New Item**. Select the **Web Form** item and provide it with the name **Add.aspx**. Click the **Add** button.

2. Open the Default.aspx page in the Solution Explorer window by double-clicking the **Default.aspx** page.

3. Switch to Design view by clicking the **Design** tab located at the bottom left of the page.

4. Add a **HyperLink** control to the Default.aspx page by dragging the control onto the page from under the Standard tab in the Toolbox window.

5. Right-click the **HyperLink** control and select the menu option **Properties**.

6. In the Properties window, modify the Text property. Assign the value **Add Employee** to the Text property.

7. In the Properties window, modify the NavigateUrl property. Assign the value **~/Add.aspx** to the NavigateUrl property.

Add the necessary data controls to the Add.aspx page:

8. Open the **Add.aspx** page in the Editor window by double-clicking the page in the Solution Explorer window.

9. Switch to Design view by clicking the **Design** tab, which appears at the bottom left of the Editor window.

10. Add a **DetailsView** control to the Add.aspx page by dragging the control from beneath the Data tab in the toolbox onto the page.

11. Open the DetailsView Tasks window by clicking the **Smart Tasks** icon, which appears at the top-right corner of the DetailsView control (or right-click the **DetailsView** control and select the menu option **Show Smart Tag**).

12. Open the **Data Source Configuration Wizard** by selecting the **<New data source>** option from **Choose Data Source** in the GridView Tasks window.

13. When prompted to **Choose a Data Source Type**, select **Database**. Click the **OK** button.

14. When prompted to **Choose Your Data Connection**, select the **EmployeesDBConnection** connection string. Click the **Next** button.

15. When prompted to **Configure Your Select Statement**, select **Specify columns from a table or view**. For **Name**, select **Employees** and for **Columns**, select * for all columns.

16. Click the **Advanced** button and check the checkbox labeled **Generate Insert, Update, and Delete statements**. Click the **OK** button and click the **Next** button.

17. When prompted to **Test Query**, click the **Finish** button.

Next, configure the DetailsView control to display the user interface required for inserting new records:

18. Open the DetailsView Tasks window by clicking the **Smart Tasks** icon, which appears at the top-right corner of the DetailsView control (or right-click the **DetailsView** control and select the menu option **Show Smart Tag**).

19. Check the checkbox labeled **Enable Inserting**.

Next, configure the DetailsView control to display in Insert mode by default:

20. Right-click the **DetailsView** control in the Editor window and select the menu option **Properties**.

21. In the Properties window, set the DefaultMode property to the value **Insert**.

Finally, add code to the DetailsView control to redirect the user back to the Default.aspx page when a new record is entered into the Employee database:

22. Right-click the **DetailsView** control in the Editor window and select the menu option **Properties**.

23. In the Properties window, click the **Events** button (the icon of the lightning bolt) to see all the events associated with the DetailsView control.

24. Double-click the **ItemInserted** event.

25. Add the following code to create the ItemInserted event handler:

```
Protected Sub DetailsView1_ItemInserted(ByVal sender As Object, _
    ByVal e As System.Web.UI.WebControls.DetailsViewInsertedEventArgs)
        Response.Redirect("~/Default.aspx")
    End Sub
```

Creating the Edit.aspx Page

The Edit.aspx Web Form page enables you to edit existing employees in the Employee Directory (see Figure 11). Follow these steps to create the Edit.aspx page.

Figure 11   Editing an existing employee in the Employee Directory.

First, modify the SqlDataSource control contained in the Default.aspx page so that it returns the Id column:

1. Open the **Default.aspx** page in the Editor window by double-clicking the page in the Solution Explorer window.

2. Switch to Design view by clicking the **Design** tab, which appears at the bottom left of the Editor window.

3. Open the SqlDataSource Tasks window by clicking the **Smart Tasks** icon, which appears at the top-right corner of the SqlDataSource control (or right-click the **SqlDataSource** control and select the menu option **Show Smart Tag**).

4. When prompted to **Choose Your Data Connection**, make no changes and click the **Next** button.

5. When prompted to **Configure Your Select Statement**, add an additional column to the columns selected. Check the checkbox next to the Id column. Click the **Next** button.

6. When prompted to **Test Query**, click the **Finish** button.

Next, modify the GridView control in the Default.aspx page so that each record links to the Edit.aspx page:

7. Open the GridView Tasks window by clicking the **Smart Tasks** icon, which appears at the top-right corner of the GridView control (or right-click the **GridView** control and select the menu option **Show Smart Tag**).

8. Click the **Edit Columns** link.

9. From **Available fields**, select the **HyperLinkField** and click the **Add** button. The HyperLinkField appears under **Selected fields**.

10. Select the new HyperLinkField under **Selected fields** and move the HyperLinkField to the top of the list of fields by repeatedly clicking the **Up** button.

11. Modify the HyperLinkField's Text property. Assign the value **Edit** to this property.

12. Modify the HyperLinkField's DataNavigateUrlFields property. Assign the value **Id** to this property.

13. Modify the HyperLinkField's DataNavigateUrlFormatString. Assign the value **~/Edit.aspx?id={0}** to this property.

Next, create the Edit.aspx page and add the necessary data controls:

14. Create the Edit.aspx page by selecting the menu option **Website**, **Add New Item**. Select the **Web Form** item and provide it with the name **Edit.aspx**. Click the **Add** button.

15. Switch to Design view by clicking the **Design** tab, which appears at the bottom left of the Editor window.

16. Add a **DetailsView** control to the Edit.aspx page by dragging the control from beneath the Data tab in the toolbox onto the page.

17. Open the DetailsView Tasks window by clicking the **Smart Tasks** icon, which appears at the top-right corner of the DetailsView control (or right-click the **DetailsView** control and select the menu option **Show Smart Tag**).

18. Open the Data Source Configuration Wizard by selecting the **<New data source>** option from **Choose Data Source** in the GridView Tasks window.

19. When prompted to **Choose a Data Source Type**, select **Database**. Click the **OK** button.

20. When prompted to **Choose Your Data Connection**, select the **EmployeesDBConnection** connection string. Click the **Next** button.

21. When prompted to **Configure Your Select Statement**, select **Specify columns from a table or view**. For **Name**, select **Employees** and for **Columns**, select * for all columns.

22. Click the **WHERE** button. For **Column**, select **Id**. For **Operator**, select =. For **Source**, select **QueryString**. For **QueryStringField**, enter **Id**. Click the **Add** button. Click the **OK** button.

23. Click the **Advanced** button and check the checkbox labeled **Generate Insert, Update, and Delete statements**. Click the **OK** button and click the **Next** button.

24. When prompted to **Test Query**, click the **Finish** button.

Next, configure the DetailsView control to display the user interface required for editing records:

25. Open the DetailsView Tasks window by clicking the **Smart Tasks** icon, which appears at the top-right corner of the DetailsView control (or right-click the **DetailsView** control and select the menu option **Show Smart Tag**).

26. Check the checkbox labeled **Enable Editing**.

Next, configure the DetailsView control to display in Edit mode by default:

27. Right-click the **DetailsView** control in the Editor window and select the menu option **Properties**.

28. In the Properties window, set the DefaultMode property to the value **Edit**.

Finally, add code to the DetailsView control to redirect the user back to the Default.aspx page when a record is modified in the Employee database:

29. Right-click the **DetailsView** control in the Editor window and select the menu option **Properties**.

30. In the Properties window, click the **Events** button (the icon of the lightning bolt) to see all the events associated with the DetailsView control.

31. Double-click the **ItemUpdated** event.

32. Add the following code to create the ItemUpdated event handler:

```
Protected Sub DetailsView1_ItemUpdated(ByVal sender As Object, _
   ByVal e As System.Web.UI.WebControls.DetailsViewUpdatedEventArgs) _
  Handles DetailsView1.ItemUpdated
        Response.Redirect("~/Default.aspx")
End Sub
```

module ▷ 3

Using the ASP.NET 2.0 Data Access Controls

In this module, you learn how to use each of the main ASP.NET 2.0 data access controls in detail. In particular, you learn how to use the List Controls to display a list of options. You also learn how to use the GridView control to display, page through, sort, and edit database records. You learn how to use both the DetailsView and FormView control to display and edit a single database record. Finally, you learn how to use the Repeater and DataList controls to provide a more specialized view of database data.

Creating the Movies and MovieCategories Database Tables

The sample pages in this lesson use a new database named MoviesDB. You create this database by selecting the menu option **Website**, **Add New Item** and selecting the **SQL Database** item. Name the new database MoviesDB.mdf and click the **OK** button. You are prompted to add the database to the App_Data folder.

After you create the MoviesDB database, you need to add two database tables to the database: a table named Movies and a table named MovieCategories. Create the Movies database table by right-clicking the **Tables** folder in the Database Explorer window (named Server Explorer in Visual Studio 2005) and selecting **Add New Table**. Add the following columns:

Column Name	Data Type	Allow Nulls
Id	int	false
Title	nvarchar(150)	false
Director	nvarchar(150)	false
DateReleased	datetime	false
CategoryId	int	false

The Id column should be marked as a primary key column. You can mark the Id column as a primary key column by clicking the icon of the key, which appears toward the top of the table editor window.

Furthermore, the Id column must be an identity column. You can mark the Id column as an identity column by expanding `Identity Specification` under `Column Properties` and setting the property `Is Identity` to the value **Yes**. An identity column generates a unique number for each row added to a table automatically.

The MovieCategories database table has the following columns:

Column Name	Data Type	Allow Nulls
Id	int	false
Name	nvarchar(50)	false

Once again, the Id column should be marked as a primary key column and it should be set as an identity column.

Next, we need to add some fake data to our database tables. Right-click the **MovieCategories** table and select the menu option **Show Table Data**. Enter the two movie categories **Drama** and **Science Fiction**. When entering the two rows, don't add a value for the Id column. The Id column gets its value automatically.

Next, open the Movies database table by selecting **Show Table Data** and add a couple of movies. (You can make up any movie data you want for your fake data.) Associate each of the movies you add with one of the two movie categories defined in the MovieCategories table (use either 1 or 2 for the value of the CategoryId column).

Using the List Controls

The List Controls consist of the `DropDownList`, `ListBox`, `RadioButtonList`, `CheckBoxList`, and `BulletedList` controls. All these controls enable you to display a list of options the user can select.

In this section, you learn how to create a simple master/detail form with a `DropDownList` control and `GridView` control (see Figure 12). The `DropDownList` control is used to display a list of movie categories. The `GridView` control displays a list of movies that match the category selected in the `DropDownList` control.

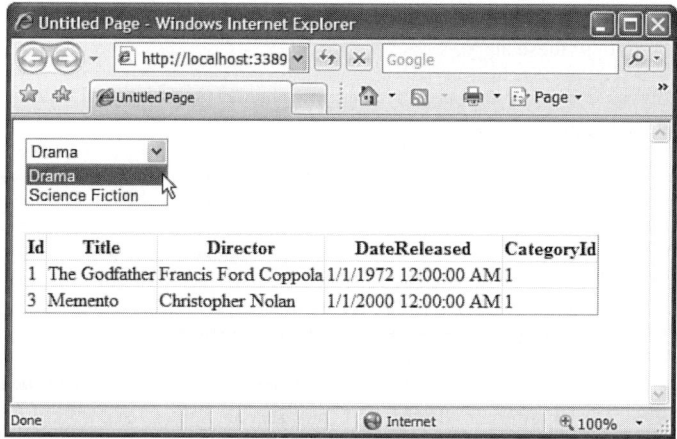

Figure 12   Creating a simple master/detail form with a `DropDownList` and a `GridView`.

Follow these steps to create a page that displays a list of options with the `DropDownList` control:

1. Create a new Web Form page named **ShowDropDownList.aspx**.

2. Switch to **Design** view.

3. Add a `DropDownList` control to the page by dragging a `DropDownList` control onto the page from beneath the Standard tab in the Toolbox.

4. In the DropDownList Tasks window, click the **Choose Data Source...** link.

5. When prompted to `Choose a Data Source`, select **<New data source>**.

6. When prompted to `Choose a Data Source Type`, select **Database**. Click the **OK** button.

7. When prompted to `Choose Your Data Connection`, click the **New Connection** button. Select **Microsoft SQL Server Database File** and click the **OK** button. Browse to the MoviesDB.mdf database file and click the **OK** button. Click the **Next** button.

8. When prompted to `Save the Connection String to the Application Configuration File`, select **Yes** and enter the name **MoviesDBConnectionString**. Click the **Next** button.

9. When prompted to `Configure the Select Statement`, select **Specify columns from a table or view**. For `Name`, select **MovieCategories** and for `Columns`, select * for all columns. Click the **Next** button.

10. When prompted to `Test Query`, click the **Finish** button.

11. Back at the Choose a Data Source dialog, select **Name** for the data field to display in the `DropDownList` and select **Id** for the data field to set the value of the `DropDownList`. Click the **OK** button.

Next, we need to add a `GridView` control to the page to display the detail records (the list of matching movies). Follow these steps:

12. Add a **GridView** control to the page by dragging the `GridView` control onto the page from beneath the Data tab in the Toolbox.

13. Open the GridView Tasks window and select **<New data source>** from **Choose Data Source**.

14. When prompted to **Select a Data Source Type**, select **Database**. Click the **Next** button.

15. When prompted to **Choose Your Data Connection**, select the existing **MoviesDBConnectionString** connection string. Click the **Next** button.

16. When prompted to **Configure the Select Statement**, select **Specify columns from a table or view**. For **Name**, enter **Movies** and for **Columns**, select * for all columns. Click the **WHERE** button. For **Column**, enter **CategoryId**, for **Operator**, select =, and for **Source**, select **Control**. For **Control Id**, enter **DropDownList1** (see Figure 13). Click the **Add** button to add the WHERE clause. Click the **OK** button. Click the **Next** button.

17. When prompted to **Test Query**, click the **Finish** button.

Finally, modify the `DropDownList` control to post the page back to the server when a new selection is made:

18. Right-click the **DropDownList** control and select the menu option **Properties**.

19. In the Properties window, set the `AutoPostBack` property to the value **True**.

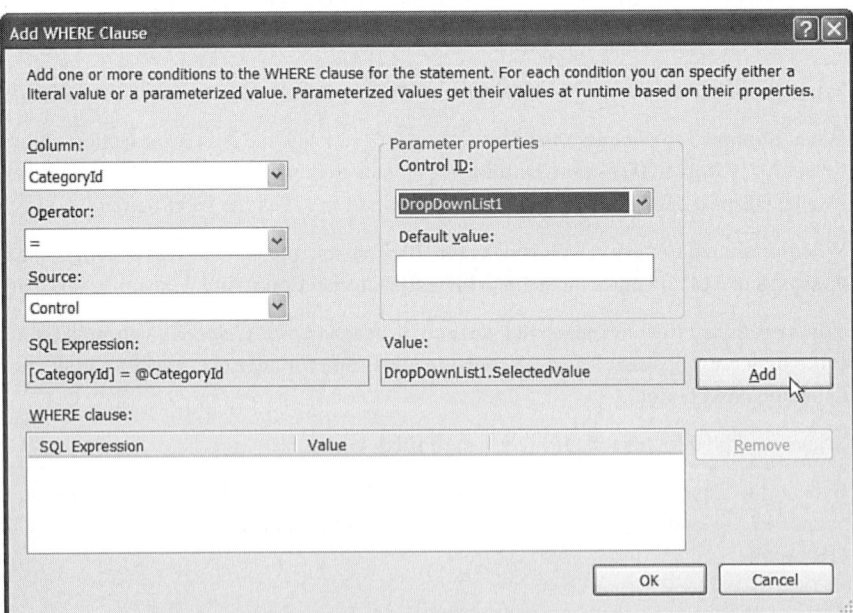

Figure 13   Linking the `DropDownList` and `GridView` controls.

Using the GridView Control

The GridView control is the main control in the ASP.NET 2.0 framework for working with a set of database records. You can use the GridView control to display, sort, page through, and edit a set of database records.

Displaying Records with the GridView Control

In this section, you learn how to display a set of database records with the GridView control. The contents of the Movies database table is shown in three easy steps (see Figure 14).

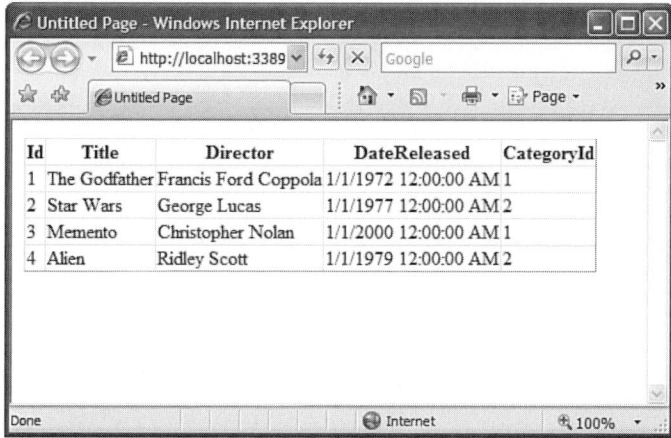

Figure 14   Displaying the contents of the Movies database table with the GridView control.

Follow these steps:

1. Create a new Web Form page named **ShowGridView.aspx**.

2. Switch to **Design** view.

3. Drag the Movies database table from the Database Explorer window onto the page (the Database Explorer window is named the Server Explorer window in the full version of Visual Studio 2005).

If you want to improve the appearance of the GridView control, there are two things you can do. First, you can pick an Auto Format scheme for the GridView control—such as Professional, Clover Field, or Snowy Pine—by opening the GridView Tasks window and clicking the **Auto Format** link. Second, you can format the appearance of particular GridView columns by opening the GridView Tasks window and clicking the **Edit Columns** link.

Sorting Records with the GridView Control

If you want to enable the viewers of a web page to change the order of the rows in a GridView, you can enable sorting. When you enable sorting, the headers in a GridView become links. When you click a particular header link, the rows are reordered by the column associated with the header link (see Figure 15).

Follow these steps to enable sorting for the ShowGridView.aspx page:

1. Open the **GridView Tasks** window.

2. Check the checkbox labeled **Enable Sorting**.

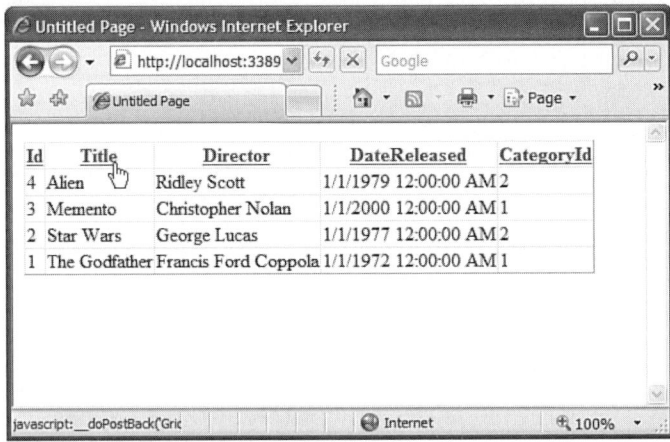

Figure 15   Sorting the rows in a GridView control by title.

Paging Through Records with the GridView Control

If you are working with a large set of database records, you should want to display the records in different pages (see Figure 16). You can page through a large set of records by enabling paging.

Follow these steps to enable paging:

1. Open the **GridView Tasks** window.

2. Check the checkbox labeled **Enable Paging**.

By default, the GridView control displays 10 database records per page. If you want to change this default, you can modify the GridView control's PageSize property in the Properties window.

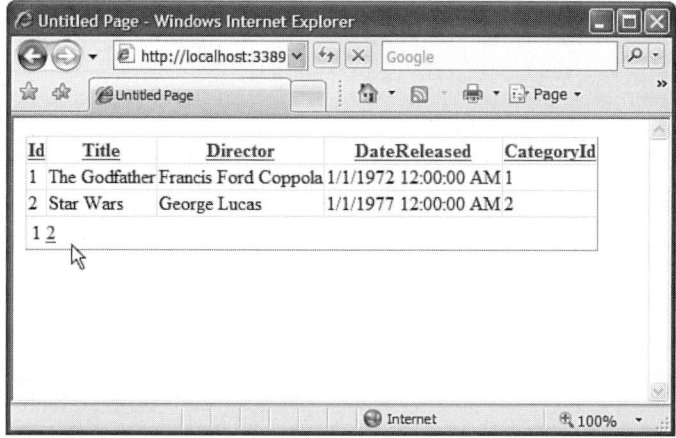

Figure 16   Paging through records with the `GridView` control.

Using Ajax with GridView Sorting and Paging

Ajax (Asynchronous JavaScript and XML) enables you to send information back and forth to a web server without posting a web page back to the web server. By taking advantage of Ajax, you can create a smoother sorting and paging experience for the user of a web page.

To enable Ajax for the `GridView` control, follow these steps:

1. Right-click the **GridView** control and select the menu option **Properties**.

2. In the Properties window, assign the value **True** to the `EnablePagingAndSortingCallbacks` property.

Enabling Ajax for the `GridView` control does not change the appearance of the `GridView` control. However, when Ajax is enabled and you sort or page through records with the `GridView` control, the page no longer posts back to the server.

Editing Records with the GridView Control

Follow these steps to modify the ShowGridView.aspx page so that you can edit and delete movie records with the page (see Figure 17).

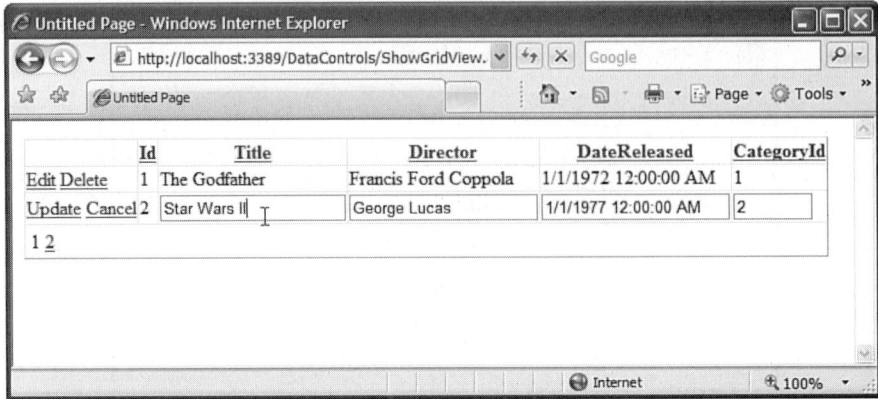

Figure 17   Editing records with the GridView control.

First, ensure the SqlDataSource control associated with the GridView is configured to support both UPDATE and DELETE statements:

1. In the GridView Tasks window, click the **Configure Data Source** link.

2. When prompted to **Choose Your Data Source**, make no changes. Click the **Next** button.

3. When prompted to **Configure the Select Statement**, click the **Advanced** button. Ensure that the checkbox labeled **Generate INSERT, UPDATE, and DELETE statements** is checked. Click the **OK** button. Click the **Next** button.

4. When prompted to **Test Query**, click the **Finish** button.

Next, modify the GridView control to generate the user interface for editing and deleting records:

Open the GridView Tasks window and check the checkbox labeled **Enable Editing** and the checkbox labeled **Enable Deleting**.

Using the DetailsView Control

The DetailsView control enables you to view, edit, insert, and delete a single database record. You can use the DetailsView control to display record details (for example, when creating a master/detail form). You also can use the DetailsView control to create both insert and edit forms for creating and modifying database records.

Paging Through Database Records with the DetailsView Control

In this section, you learn how to use the DetailsView control to page through all the records in the Movies database table (see Figure 18).

Figure 18   Paging through database records with the DetailsView control.

First, follow these steps to display a single database record with the DetailsView control:

1. Create a new Web Form page named **ShowDetailsView.aspx**.

2. Switch to **Design** view.

3. Open the **DetailsView Tasks** window and select **<New data source>** from **Choose Data Source**.

4. When prompted to **Choose a Data Source Type**, select **Database**. Click the **OK** button.

5. When prompted to **Choose Your Data Connection**, select the **MoviesDBConnectionString** connection string. Click the **Next** button.

6. When prompted to **Configure the Select Statement**, select **Specify columns from a table or view**. For **Name**, select **Movies** and for **Columns** select * to select all columns. Click the **Next** button.

7. When prompted to **Test Query**, click the **Finish** button.

At this point, the DetailsView control retrieves all the movies from the Movies database table and it displays only a single record. If you want to page through the records in the Movies database table with the DetailsView control, you need to enable paging:

8. Open the **DetailsView Tasks** window and select the **Enable Paging** checkbox.

After paging is enabled, you can navigate to all the records contained in the Movies database table.

Creating a Master/Detail Form with the DetailsView Control

In this section, we create a master/detail form with a GridView control and a DetailsView control. The first page contains a GridView control that displays a list of records as links. When you click a record, you are transferred to a second page that displays record details. The second page is implemented with a `DetailsView` control (see Figure 19).

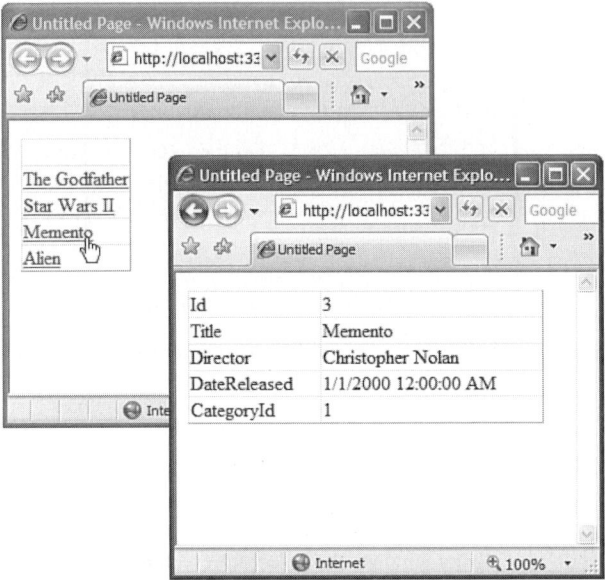

Figure 19   Creating a master/detail form with a `GridView` control and a `DetailsView` control.

Let's start by creating the master page and adding `GridView` and `SqlDataSource` controls to the page:

1. Create a new Web Form page named **Master.aspx**.

2. Switch to **Design** view.

3. Add a `GridView` control to the page by dragging the control onto the page from beneath the Data tab in the Toolbox window.

4. Open the **GridView Tasks** window and select **<New data source>** from **Choose Data Source**.

5. When prompted to `Choose a Data Source Type`, select **Database**. Click the **OK** button.

6. When prompted to `Choose Your Data Connection`, select the **MoviesDBConnectionString** connection string. Click the **Next** button.

7. When prompted to `Configure the Select Statement`, select **Specify columns from a table or view**. For `Name`, select **Movies** and for `Columns` select the **Title** and **Id** columns. Click the **Next** button.

8. When prompted to `Test Query`, click the **Finish** button.

Next, you need to modify the master page so that the `GridView` displays the list of movie records as links:

9. Open the **GridView Tasks** window and click the **Edit Columns** link.

10. From under `Selected fields`, remove both the **Id** and **Title** fields by clicking the **Delete** button (the big red X).

11. From under `Available fields`, select the **HyperLinkField** and click the **Add** button.

12. Modify the properties for the HyperLinkField. Set the `DataTextField` property to the value **Title**. Set the `DataNavigateUrlFields` property to the value **Id**. Set the `DataNavigateUrlFormatString` property to the value **~/Details.aspx?id={0}**.

13. Close the Edit Fields dialog box by clicking the **OK** button.

Next, we need to create the details page that contains the `DetailsView` control:

14. Create a new Web Form page named **Details.aspx**.

15. Switch to **Design** view.

16. Drag a `DetailsView` control onto the page by dragging it from underneath the Data tab in the Toolbox.

17. Open the **DetailsView Tasks** window and select **<New data source>** from `Choose Data Source`.

18. When prompted to `Choose a Data Source Type`, select **Database**. Click the **OK** button.

19. When prompted to `Choose Your Data Connection`, select the **MoviesDBConnectionString** connection string. Click the **Next** button.

20. When prompted to `Configure the Select Statement`, select **Specify columns from a table or view**. For `Name`, select **Movies** and for `Columns` select * for all columns. Click the **WHERE** button. For `Column` select **Id**, for `Operator` select =, and for `Source` select **QueryString**. For `QueryString field`, enter **Id**. Click the **Add** button to add the WHERE clause. Click the **OK** button. Click the **Next** button.

21. When prompted to `Test Query`, click the **Finish** button.

If you open the Master.aspx page in your browser, you can click any of the links and view the detailed movie record with the `DetailsView` control.

Editing with the DetailsView Control

In this section, you learn how to edit, insert, and delete database records with the `DetailsView` control. You learn how to modify the ShowDetailsView.aspx page we created earlier so that it supports this editing functionality (see Figure 20).

Figure 20   Editing a record with the DetailsView control.

First, we need to modify the SqlDataSource control associated with the DetailsView control so that it supports updating, inserting, and deleting commands:

1. If the ShowDetailsView.aspx page is not already open in the Editor window, double-click the page in the Solution Explorer window.

2. Open the **DetailsView Tasks** and click the **Configure Data Source** link.

3. When prompted to **Choose Your Data Connection**, don't make any changes. Click the **Next** button.

4. When prompted to **Configure the Select Statement**, click the **Advanced** button. Ensure the checkbox labeled **Generate INSERT, UPDATE, and DELETE statement** is checked and click the **OK** button. Click the **Next** button.

5. When prompted to **Test Query**, click the **Finish** button.

Next, you need to modify the DetailsView control so that it displays the user interface for editing, inserting, and deleting data.

6. Open the **DetailsView Tasks** window and check the checkboxes labeled **Enable Editing**, **Enable Inserting**, and **Enable Deleting**.

Using the FormView Control

The FormView control can be used in exactly the same scenarios as the DetailsView control. You can use the FormView control to display, edit, insert, and delete single database records. Just like the DetailsView control, you can use the FormView control to create master/details forms. You can also use the FormView control to create insert and edit forms.

Unlike the `DetailsView` control, however, the `FormView` control is completely template driven. This means you can use the `FormView` control to create more complicated website forms. When building websites for the real world, you end up using the `FormView` control much more often than the `DetailsView` control.

Displaying Database Records with the FormView Control

In this section, you learn how to display a database record with the `FormView` control. You learn how to modify the `FormView` control's item template to customize the appearance of the record.

First, you need to create a new page and add the `FormView` control to the page:

1. Create a new Web Form page named **ShowFormView.aspx**.

2. Switch to **Design** view.

3. Drag a **FormView** control onto the page by dragging the control from beneath the Data tab in the Toolbox window onto the page.

4. Open the **FormView Tasks** window.

5. Select **<New data source>** from **Choose Data Source**.

6. When prompted to **Choose a Data Source Type**, select **Database**. Click the **OK** button.

7. When prompted to **Choose Your Data Connection**, select the **MoviesDBConnectionString** connection string. Click the **Next** button.

8. When prompted to **Configure the Select Statement**, select **Specify columns from a table or view**. For **Name**, select **Movies** and for **Columns** select * to select all columns. Click the **Next** button.

9. When prompted to **Test Query**, click the **Finish** button.

Next, you can customize the way the `FormView` control renders a database record:

10. Open the **FormView Tasks** window.

11. Click the **Edit Templates** link.

12. Select **ItemTemplate** from the list of templates.

13. Click the **ItemTemplate** and modify the contents of the item template (see Figure 21). For example, you can format the label for each of the database fields by making each label bold (select a label and select the menu option **Format**, **Font**, **Bold**).

14. When you finish editing the item template, open the **FormView Tasks** window and click the **End Template Editing** link.

When you use a `FormView` control, you can format the contents of the item template in whatever way you please. This flexibility of formatting is the primary advantage of the `FormView` control over the `DetailsView` control.

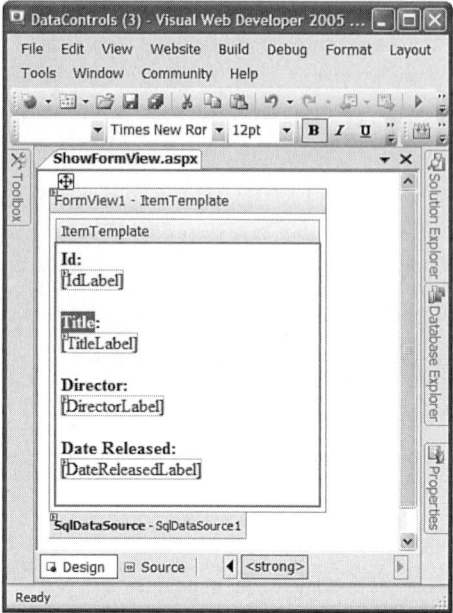

Figure 21   Modifying the FormView control's item template.

Right now, the FormView control displays only a single record regardless of the number of records retrieved from the database. If you want to page through multiple records, you can enable paging for the FormView control:

15. Open the **FormView Tasks** window.

16. Select the checkbox labeled `Enable Paging`.

After you enable paging, you can click a page number to navigate directly to a particular database record (see Figure 22).

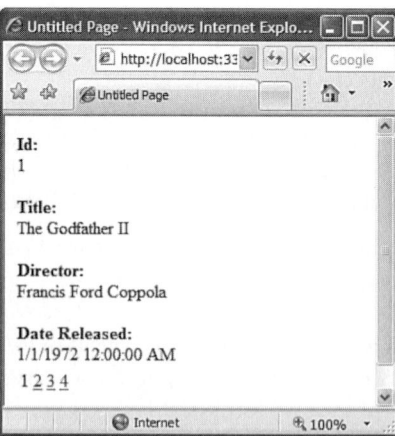

Figure 22   Paging through database records with the FormView control.

Editing Database Records with the FormView Control

In this section, you learn how to edit database records with the FormView control. In particular, you learn how to edit existing database records and add new database records. When you use a FormView control to edit records, you can customize the form for editing records in anyway you please.

Follow these steps to configure the SqlDataSource associated with the FormView control to support editing:

1. If the **ShowFormView.aspx** page is not already open, double-click the page in the Solution Explorer window.

2. Switch to **Design** view.

3. Open the **FormView Tasks** window.

4. Click the **Configure Data Source** link.

5. When prompted to **Choose Your Data Connection**, don't make any changes. Click the **Next** button.

6. When prompted to **Configure the Select Statement**, click the **Advanced** button. Ensure the checkbox labeled **Generate INSERT, UPDATE, and DELETE statements** is checked. Click the **OK** button. Click the **Next** button.

7. When prompted to **Test Query**, click the **Finish** button.

Follow these steps to add a link to the FormView to switch it into Edit mode:

8. Open the **FormView Tasks** window.

9. Click the **Edit Templates** link.

10. Select the **ItemTemplate**.

11. Drag a LinkButton from under the Standard tab in the Toolbox onto the FormView control's item template.

12. Modify the LinkButton control's Text property. Set the Text property to the value **Edit Movie**.

13. Modify the LinkButton control's **CommandName** property. Set the CommandName property to the value **Edit**.

14. Click the link labeled **End Template Editing** in the FormView Tasks window.

After you complete these steps, you can click the Edit link to edit an existing record with the FormView control (see Figure 23).

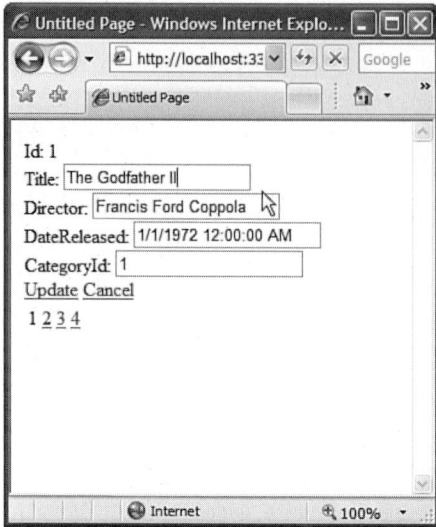

Figure 23   Editing an existing record with the FormView control.

Follow these steps to add a link to the FormView to switch it into Insert mode:

15. Open the **FormView Tasks** window.

16. Click the **Edit Templates** link.

17. Select the **ItemTemplate**.

18. Drag a LinkButton from under the Standard tab in the Toolbox onto the FormView control's item template.

19. Modify the LinkButton control's Text property. Set the Text property to the value **New Movie**.

20. Modify the LinkButton control's **CommandName** property. Set the CommandName property to the value **New**.

21. Click the link labeled **End Template Editing** in the FormView Tasks window.

After you complete these steps, you can click the **New** link to add a new record with the FormView control (see Figure 24).

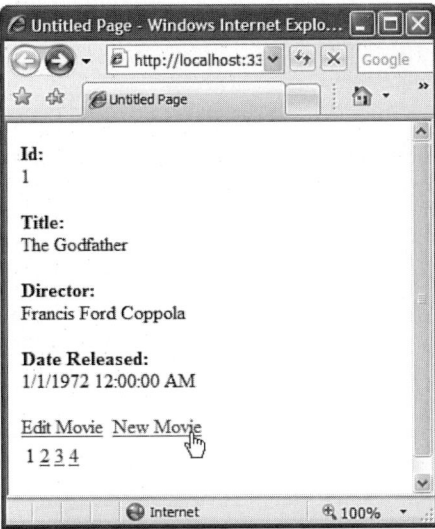

Figure 24   Adding a new record with the `FormView` control.

Using the FormView Control with Validation Controls

Typically, when you display a form on a web page, you want to validate the data into the form before submitting the data to a database. For example, certain form fields can be required fields. In this section, you learn how to validate the form fields displayed by the `FormView` control.

Follow these steps:

1. Open the **FormView Tasks** window.

2. Click the **Edit Templates** link.

3. Select the **EditItemTemplate** as the template to edit.

4. Drag a `RequiredFieldValidator` control from beneath the Validation tab in the Toolbox onto the `FormView` control's edit item template. Place the `RequiredFieldValidator` control right next to the Title form field (if you need more room, you can stretch the `FormView` so that it is wider).

5. Set two properties of the `RequiredFieldValidator` control. Set the `Text` property to the value **Required!** and set the `ControlToValidate` property to the value **TitleTextBox**.

6. Click the **End Template Editing** link in the FormView Tasks window.

After you complete these steps, you receive an error message if you attempt to edit a movie and you do not enter a movie title (see Figure 25).

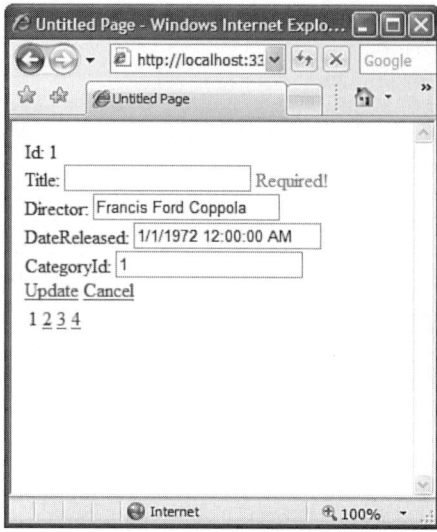

Figure 25   Attempting to update a movie without supplying a movie title.

Using a FormView Control with a DropDownList Control

By default, when you bind a `FormView` control to a `SqlDataSource` control, the `FormView` control creates a `TextBox` for each database field in its data source. Sometimes, you want to use form fields other than `TextBox` controls with a `FormView` control. For example, it would be nice if our `FormView` control would display a `DropDownList` for selecting a movie category when you add a new movie or edit an existing movie (see Figure 26). Because it would be nice, let's do it.

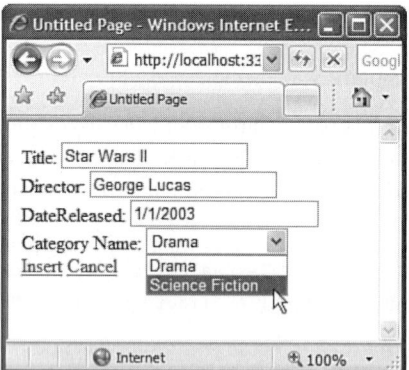

Figure 26   Using a `DropDownList` control when adding a new movie.

Follow these steps to modify the `FormView` control so that it displays a `DropDownList` of movie categories when you add a new movie:

1. Open the **FormView Tasks** window.

2. Click the **Edit Templates** link.

3. Select the **InsertItemTemplate**.

4. Delete the **Category Id** label and `TextBox` controls from the `FormView` control's insert item template.

5. Add a `DropDownList` control to the InsertItemTemplate by dragging the control from beneath the Standard tab in the Toolbox window and dropping it in the insert item template.

6. Open the **DropDownList Tasks** window.

7. Click the **Choose Data Source** link.

8. Select **<New data source>** from `Choose a Data Source`.

9. When prompted to `Choose a Data Source Type`, select **Database**. Click the **OK** button.

10. When prompted to `Choose Your Data Connection`, select the **MoviesDBConnectionString** connection string. Click the **Next** button.

11. When prompted to `Configure the Select Statement`, select **Specify columns from a table or view**. For `Name`, select **MovieCategories** and for `Columns`, select **Id** and **Name**. Click the **Next** button.

12. When prompted to `Test Query`, click the **Finish** button.

13. Back at the Choose a Data Source dialog box, select **Name** for the data field to display and **Id** for the value of the `DropDownList`. Click the **OK** button.

Finally, you must bind the `SelectedValue` property of the `DropDownList` control to the CategoryId column from the MovieCategories database table. Follow these steps:

14. Open the **DropDownList Tasks** window.

15. Click the **Edit DataBindings** link.

16. Under `Bindable Properties`, select the `SelectedValue` property.

17. From the `Bound to` drop-down list, select the **CategoryId** database column.

18. Click the **OK** button.

After you complete these steps, you can select a movie category from a drop-down list when adding a new movie record to the Movies database table.

Using the Repeater Control

The `Repeater` control, like the `GridView` control, enables you to display a set of database records. However, unlike the `GridView` control, the `Repeater` control is completely template driven. This means you can completely customize the layout of the database records displayed by the `Repeater` control.

Follow these steps to display the contents of the Movies database table with a `Repeater` control:

1. Create a new Web Form page named **ShowRepeater.aspx**.

2. Switch to **Design** view.

3. Drag a `Repeater` control onto the page by dragging the control from beneath the Data tab in the Toolbox window.

4. Open the **Repeater Tasks** window and select **<New data source>** from `Choose Data Source`.

5. When prompted to `Choose a Data Source Type`, select **Database**. Click the **OK** button.

6. When prompted to `Choose Your Data Connection`, select the **MoviesDBConnectionString** connection string. Click the **Next** button.

7. When prompted to `Configure the Select Statement`, select **Specify columns from a table or view**. For `Name`, select **Movies** and for `Columns`, select ***** to select all the columns. Click the **Next** button.

8. When prompted to `Test Query`, click the **Finish** button.

Create the item template for the `Repeater` control by following these steps:

9. Switch to Source view by clicking the **Source** tab at the bottom left of the Editor window.

10. Find the opening and closing tags for the `Repeater` control and add the following **ItemTemplate**:

```
<asp:Repeater ID="Repeater1" runat="server" DataSourceID="SqlDataSource1">
<ItemTemplate>
  <%# Eval("Title") %>
  <hr />
</ItemTemplate>
</asp:Repeater>
```

After you complete these steps, the `Repeater` control renders all the values of the Title column for all the movie records. Below each record, a horizontal rule appears (see Figure 27).

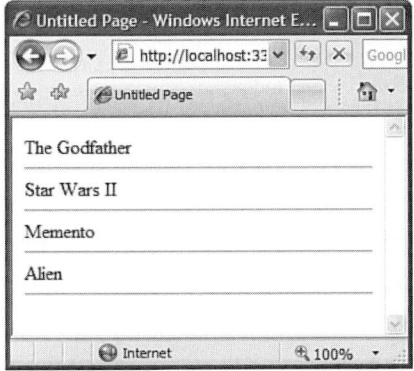

Figure 27   Displaying movies with the `Repeater` control.

Using the DataList Control

Like the `GridView` control, the `DataList` control enables you to display a set of database records. Unlike the `GridView` control, the `DataList` control displays database records in multiple columns (see Figure 28).

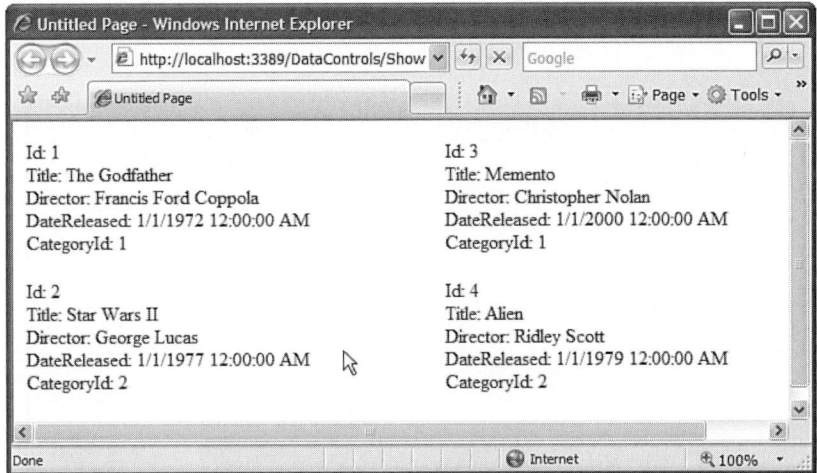

Figure 28   Displaying movie records in multiple columns.

Follow these steps to add the `DataList` control to a page:

1. Create a new Web Form page named **ShowDataList.aspx**.

2. Switch to **Design** view.

3. Drag a **DataList** control onto the page by dragging the control from beneath the Data tab in the Toolbox window.

4. Open the **DataList Tasks** window and select **<New data source>** from **Choose Data Source**.

5. When prompted to **Choose a Data Source Type**, select **Database**. Click the **OK** button.

6. When prompted to **Choose Your Data Connection**, select the **MoviesDBConnectionString** connection string. Click the **Next** button.

7. When prompted to **Configure the Select Statement**, select **Specify columns from a table or view**. For **Name**, select **Movies** and for **Columns**, select * to select all the columns. Click the **Next** button.

8. When prompted to **Test Query**, click the **Finish** button.

Follow these steps to configure the DataList to display multiple columns:

9. Right-click the **DataList** control and select the menu option **Properties**.

10. In the Properties window, set the Repeat Columns property to the value **2**.

As an alternative to setting the number of columns displayed by the DataList in the Properties window, you can use the DataList Property Builder. You open the Property Builder by opening the **DataList Tasks** window and clicking the **Property Builder** link. The Property Builder dialog includes a number of properties you can set to modify the formatting of a DataList control (see Figure 29).

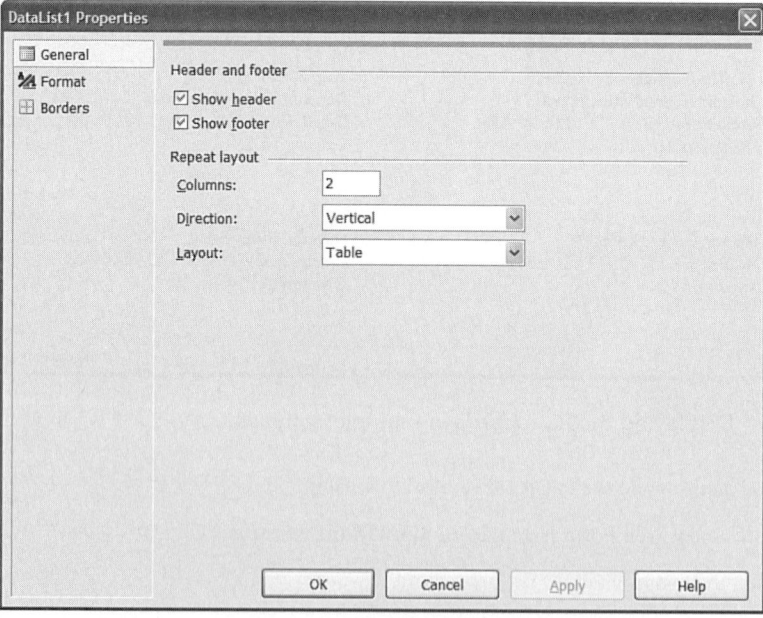

Figure 29   Adding the DataList control Property Builder dialog box.

module ▶ 4

Advanced Topics

In this lesson, you learn how to handle two problems that are inescapable in production applications. First, you learn how to handle errors gracefully. You learn how to display a custom error message when an error is encountered when accessing the database. Next, you learn how to prevent concurrency issues. You learn how to prevent two people updating a record at the same time from accidentally overwriting each other's changes.

Handling Database Errors Gracefully

In this section, you learn how to handle errors gracefully when declaratively adding ASP.NET controls to a page.

Follow these steps to create a page that displays the contents of the Movies database table:

1. Create a new Web Form page named **ShowError.aspx**.

2. Switch to **Design** view.

3. Drag the **Movies** database table from the Database Explorer window and drop it onto the ShowError.aspx page. (The Database Explorer window is called the Server Explorer window in the full version of Visual Studio 2005.)

Follow these steps to modify the SqlDataSource control so that it generates an error:

4. Open the **SqlDataSource Tasks** window.

5. Click the **Configure Data Source** link.

6. When prompted to **Choose Your Data Connection**, don't make any changes. Click the **Next** button.

7. When prompted to **Configure the Select Statement**, select **Specify a custom SQL select statement or stored procedure**. Click the **Next** button.

   Modify the SQL SELECT statement so that it refers to a nonexistent column named DoesNotExist like this:

   ```
   SELECT DoesNotExist, [Id], [Title], [Director], [DateReleased], [CategoryId]
   FROM [Movies]
   ```

Click the **Next** button.

8. When prompted to `Test Query`, click the **Finish** button.

If you open the ShowError.aspx page now, you see the angry, yellow page in Figure 30. (This book is printed in black and white, so the page won't appear yellow in the figure unless you color over the figure with a highlighter.)

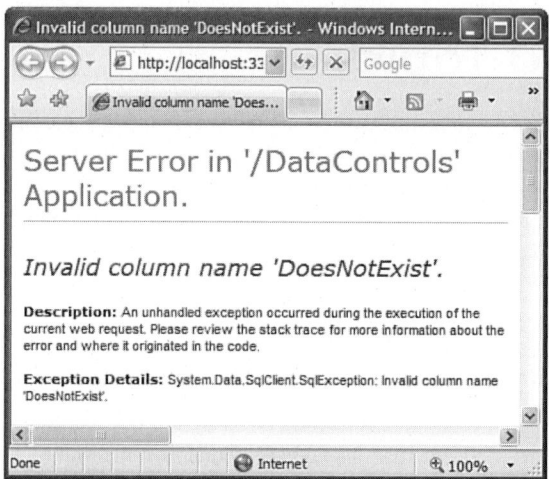

Figure 30   Displaying an ugly, yellow exception page.

Follow these steps to display a custom error message:

9. Right-click the `SqlDataSource` control and select the menu option **Properties**.

10. In the Properties window, click the **Events** button (the button with the picture of the lightning bolt).

11. Double-click the **Selected** event.

12. Add the following code to the `SqlDataSource` control's Selected event handler:

```
Protected Sub SqlDataSource1_Selected(ByVal sender As Object, _
   ByVal e As System.Web.UI.WebControls.SqlDataSourceStatusEventArgs)
      If Not IsNothing(e.Exception) Then
         lblError.Text = "There was a problem selecting records"
         e.ExceptionHandled = True
      End If
   End Sub
```

13. Add a `Label` control to the page by dragging the **Label** control from beneath the Standard tab onto the page (you can do this in Source view). Change the ID of the `Label` to the value **lblError**. Add an **EnableViewState= "false"** attribute to the `Label` control and remove any value from its `Text` property.

After you complete these steps, the custom error message `There was a problem selecting records` is displayed instead of the default angry error page (see Figure 31).

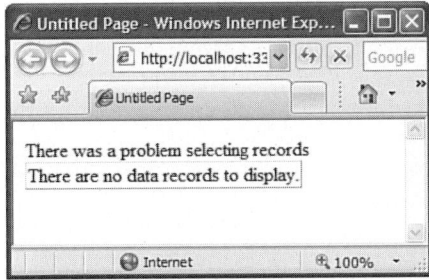

Figure 31   Displaying a custom error message.

Handling Concurrency Issues

If more than one person attempts to update the same database record at the same time, one person can accidentally overwrite another person's changes. The ASP.NET framework provides you with a way to handle this type of concurrency problem in a graceful manner.

First, create a page that displays the records from the Movies database table:

1. Create a new Web Form page named **ShowConcurrency.aspx**.

2. Switch to **Design** view.

3. Drag the **Movies** database table onto the page by dragging the table from the Database Explorer window (the Database Explorer window is called the Server Explorer window in the full version of Visual Studio 2005).

4. Open the GridView Tasks window and select the checkbox labeled `Enable Editing`.

Next, configure the data source to handle concurrency:

5. Open the **SqlDataSource Task** window.

6. Click the **Configure Data Source** link.

7. When prompted to `Choose Your Data Connection`, don't make any changes. Click the **Next** button.

8. When prompted to `Configure the Select Statement`, click the **Advanced** button. Select the **Use optimistic concurrency** checkbox (see Figure 32). Click the **OK** button. Click the **Next** button.

9. When prompted to `Test Query`, click the **Finish** button.

Modify the page so that it displays an error message when a concurrency conflict occurs:

10. Add a `Label` control to the page by dragging the control from beneath the Standard tab in the Toolbox window onto the page.

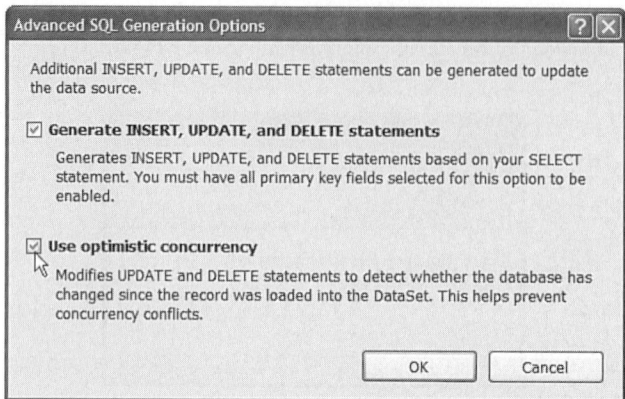

Figure 32   Enabling optimistic concurrency.

11. Right-click the **SqlDataSource** control and select the menu option **Properties**.

12. In the Properties window, click the **Events** button (the button with the lightning bolt).

13. Double-click next to the **Updated** item in the Properties window.

14. Enter the following code for the SqlDataSource control's Updated event handler:

```
Protected Sub SqlDataSource1_Updated(ByVal sender As Object, _
ByVal e As System.Web.UI.WebControls.SqlDataSourceStatusEventArgs)
     If e.AffectedRows = 0 Then
         Label1.Text = "No records were updated!"
     End If
End Sub
```

After you complete these steps, if two people attempt to change the same record at the same time, the message **No records were updated!** is displayed to the slowest of the two people attempting to perform the update (see Figure 33).

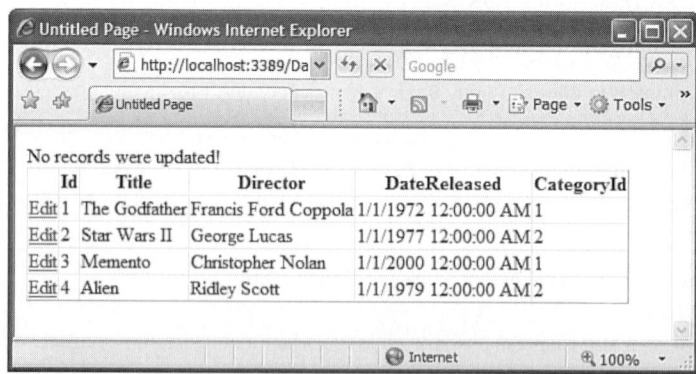

Figure 33   Displaying an error message triggered by a concurrency violation.

module ⊙ 5

Creating a Guestbook Application

In this final module, you learn how to build an entire database-driven Guestbook application (see Figure 34). This final application includes several advanced features such as pop-up JavaScript windows. Follow these steps to create the application.

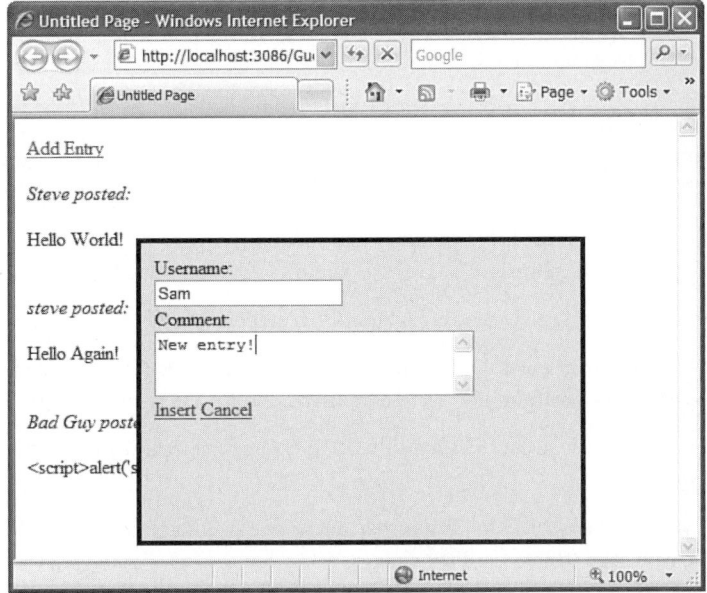

Figure 34   Adding an entry to the Guestbook application.

First, create the Guestbook website and database:

1. Select the menu option **File, New Web Site**. Select the **ASP.NET Web Site Template** for the Template, select **File System** for the Location, and select **Visual Basic** for the Language. Click the **OK** button.

2. Create a new database by selecting the menu option **Website, Add New Item**. Select the **SQL Database** template and name the database **GuestbookDB.mdf**. Click the **Add** button (when prompted, save the database to the **App_Data** folder).

3. Add a table named **Guestbook** to the database. In the Database Explorer window (named the Server Explorer window in the full version of Visual Studio 2005), right-click the **Tables** folder and select **Add New Table**. Enter the following columns:

Column Name	Data Type	Allow Nulls
Id	int	false
Username	nvarchar(300)	false
Comment	ntext	false
DateCreated	datetime	false

The Id column is a primary key column and an identity column. The DateCreated column has the default value `GetDate()`.

Next, follow these steps to add a pop-up window to the Default.aspx page:

4. If the Default.aspx page is not already open in the Editor window, double-click the page in the Solution Explorer window.

5. Switch to **Design** view.

6. Add an HTML div tag to the page by double-clicking the **Div** tag in the Toolbox window underneath the HTML tab.

7. Select the **Div** tag in the Editor window and modify its `Style` property by clicking the button labeled with the **ellipsis**. Clicking this button opens the Style Builder dialog box.

8. In the Style Builder, select the **Background** tab and change the background color to **Aqua**.

9. In the Style Builder, select the **Position** tab and change the `Position` mode property to the value **Absolutely position**. For `Top`, enter **100px** and for `Left`, enter **100px**.

10. In the Style Builder, select the **Layout** tab and change the `Display` property to the value **Do not display**.

11. In the Style Builder, select the **Edges** tab and set the padding to the value **10px** for the `Top`, `Bottom`, `Left`, and `Right`. For the `Borders`, select **Solid Line**. For the `Width`, select **Medium**. For `Color`, select **Black**.

12. Click the **OK** button to close the Style Builder.

Add a `FormView` control to the pop-up window and configure its data source:

13. Drag a **FormView** control from beneath the Data tab in the Toolbox and add the control to the **Div** tag in the Editor window.

14. Open the **FormView Tasks** window.

15. Select **<New data source>** from `Choose Data Source`.

16. When prompted to `Choose a Data Source Type`, select **Database**. Click the **OK** button.

17. When prompted to `Choose Your Data Connection`, select the **GuestbookDB.mdf** connection. Click the **Next** button.

18. When prompted to `Save the Connection String to the Application Configuration File`, select **Yes** and name the connection string **Guestbook**. Click the **Next** button.

19. When prompted to `Configure the Select Statement`, select **Specify columns from a table or view**. For `Name`, select **Guestbook** and for `Columns` select **Id**, **Username**, and **Comment**. Click the **Advanced** button and select **Generate INSERT, UPDATE, and DELETE statements**. Click the **OK** button. Click the **Next** button.

20. When prompted to `Test Query`, click the **Finish** button.

Next, modify the `FormView` control's InsertItemTemplate so that it appears by default and it has the right form fields:

21. Right-click the `FormView` control and select **Properties**.

22. In the Properties window, set the `DefaultMode` property to the value **Insert**.

23. Open the **FormView Tasks** window.

24. Click the **Edit Templates** link.

25. Select **InsertItemTemplate** from the list of templates.

26. Right-click the **Comment TextBox** and select the menu option **Properties**.

27. In the Properties window, set the `TextMode` property to the value **Multiline**.

28. In the Properties window, set the `Columns` property to the value **30**.

29. In the Properties window, set the `Rows` property to the value **3**.

Next, add validation controls to the Guestbook form:

30. Add two `RequiredFieldValidator` controls to the `FormView` control's insert item template by dragging both controls from under the Validation tab in the Toolbox window.

31. Position the first **RequiredFieldValidator** next to the Username `TextBox`.

32. Right-click the first **RequiredFieldValidator** and select the menu option **Properties**.

33. In the Properties window, and set the `Text` property to the value **(Required)** and set the `ControlToValidate` property to the value **UsernameTextBox**.

34. Position the second **RequiredFieldValidator** next to the Comment `TextBox`.

35. Right-click the second **RequiredFieldValidator** and select the menu option **Properties**.

36. In the Properties window, set the `Text` property to the value **(Required)** and set the `ControlToValidate` property to the value **CommentTextBox**.

Add a link to the page that causes the popup window to appear:

37. Right-click the **Div** tag in the Editor window and select the menu option **Properties**.

38. Set the Id property to the value **divForm**.

39. Switch to Source view by clicking on the **Source** tab, which appears at the bottom left of the Editor window.

40. Just before closing the </div> tag and closing the </form> tag, add the following hyperlink:

```
<a href="javascript:void(0)" _
   onclick="document.getElementById('divForm').style.display='block';">Add _
Entry</a>
```

Next, add a Repeater control to the Default.aspx to display all the Guestbook entries:

41. Switch to **Design** view.

42. Drag a **Repeater** control onto the page from under the Data tab in the Toolbox window.

43. Open the **Repeater Tasks** window and select **SqlDataSource1** from Choose Data Source.

44. Switch to **Source** view and find the opening and closing <asp:Repeater> tags.

45. Add the following ItemTemplate to the Repeater control:

```
<asp:Repeater ID="Repeater1" runat="server" DataSourceID="SqlDataSource1">
<ItemTemplate>
    <em><%# Eval("Username") %> posted:</em>
    <br />
    <p><%# Eval("Comment") %></p>
    </ItemTemplate>
<SeparatorTemplate>
     <br />
</SeparatorTemplate>
</asp:Repeater>
```

If you want to allow users to submit content that can resemble script or HTML tags in a safe way, perform the following modifications to the Default.aspx page:

46. Add a **ValidateRequest= "false"** attribute to the <%@ Page %> directive, which appears at the top of the Default.aspx page in Source view.

47. Modify the Repeater control so that it looks like this:

```
<asp:Repeater ID="Repeater1" runat="server" DataSourceID="SqlDataSource1">
<ItemTemplate>
    <em><%# Server.HTMLEncode(Eval("Username")) %> posted:</em>
    <br />
    <p><%# Server.HTMLEncode(Eval("Comment")) %></p>
    </ItemTemplate>
```

```
<SeparatorTemplate>
      <br />
</SeparatorTemplate>
</asp:Repeater>
```

The modified `Repeater` control's ItemTemplate now includes a call to the `Server.HTMLEncode()` method. This method escapes characters such as the < and > characters, so they can safely be displayed in a browser.

bonus ⊙ 1

An Introduction to SQL: The Language of Databases

Typically, any information stored by a website is stored in a database. There are many popular databases, including Oracle 10g, IBM DB2, MySQL, Microsoft Access, Microsoft FoxPro, and Microsoft SQL Server.

You can use a database to store as much or as little information as you like. For example, you can use a database to store a couple of recipes. Or, if you are responsible for the Amazon website, you can use a database to store terabytes of data (information on every product available).

I assume in the video that you are using Microsoft SQL Server 2005. However, every major database speaks the same language. You retrieve records from a database, and you modify records in a database by using SQL (the Structured Query Language).

Because you need to know the basics of SQL to take advantage of the ASP.NET 2.0 data access controls, I've included a brief introduction to SQL in the following pages.

Executing SQL Commands

There are a number of different ways that you can execute SQL commands. If you are using the ASP.NET data access controls, you'll typically use the `SqlDataSource` control to represent and execute SQL commands from within your ASP.NET pages. You learn how to use the `SqlDataSource` control in detail in the video.

On the other hand, if you want to execute SQL commands directly against a database, without building an ASP.NET page, you have two options. First, you can execute SQL commands within Microsoft Visual Web Developer 2005 or Microsoft Visual Studio 2005. After creating or opening a project, select the menu option View Database Explorer (this menu option is named View Server Explorer in the full version of Visual Studio 2005). Within the Database Explorer window, right-click a data connection and select the menu option **New Query**. The Query Designer will open in the main editor window (see Figure 35).

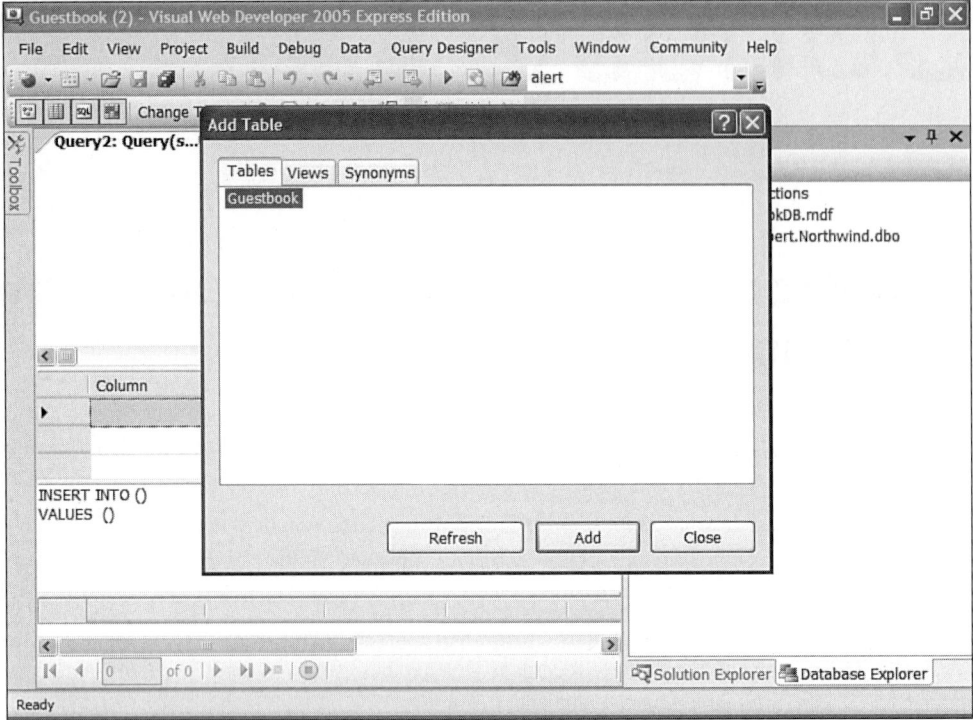

Figure 35   The Query Designer window.

When the Query Designer first opens, a dialog appears that asks you to add one or more database tables. Select a database table and click the **Add** button. Next, click the **Close** button to close the Add Table dialog box.

The main Query Designer window consists of four panes: the Diagram Pane, the Criteria Pane, the SQL Pane, and the Results Pane. You can execute SQL commands by typing the commands directly into the SQL Pane and clicking the Execute SQL button (the button with the red exclamation mark). The results of the SQL command appear in the Results pane.

For example, if you want to retrieve all the records from the Guestbook table, you would enter the following SQL command in the SQL Pane:

```
SELECT * FROM Guestbook
```

When you click the Execute SQL button, the results of this query appear in the Results Pane (see Figure 36).

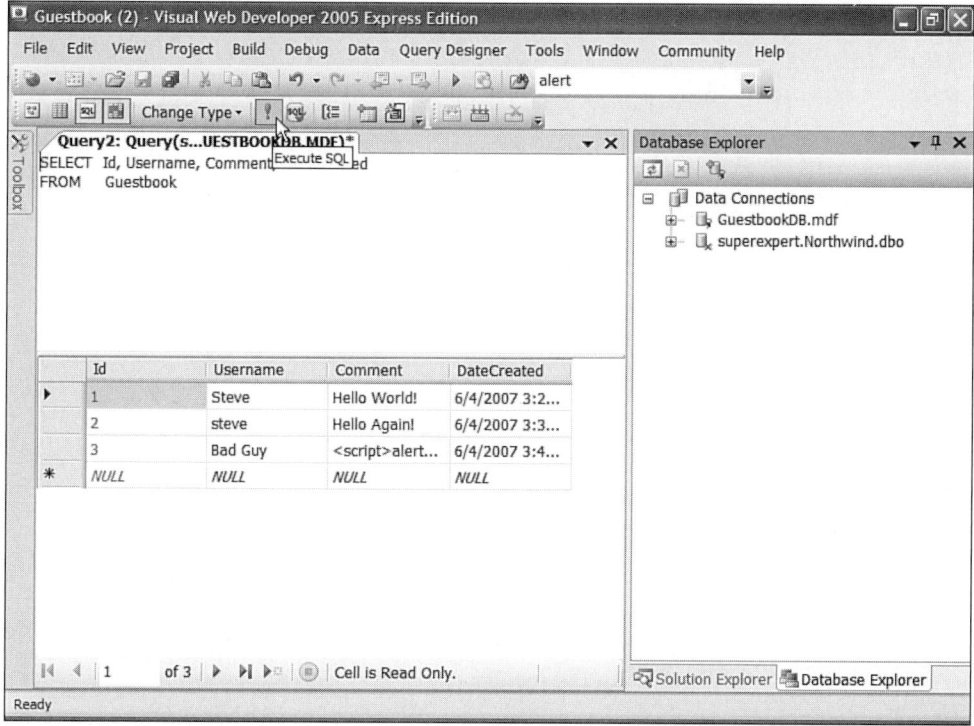

Figure 36   Displaying the results of a query.

As an alternative to using Visual Web Developer or Visual Studio to execute SQL commands, you can use Microsoft SQL Server Management Studio. If you installed the full version of Microsoft SQL Server 2005, the Management Studio is also installed. If you are using the Express edition of Microsoft SQL Server 2005, you will need to download SQL Server Management Studio Express from the Microsoft website (it's a free download).

Here's how you use Management Studio. After you launch Management Studio, the Connect to Server dialog appears. Enter the name of your database server and your credentials and click the **Login** button. (If you don't know this information, you'll need to ask your database administrator.)

Next, you can execute a SQL command against a particular database by expanding the Database folder, right-clicking a particular database, and selecting the menu option **New Query**. Selecting this menu option opens the New Query window (see Figure 37). Enter a SQL command and click the button labeled **Execute** to execute the command (or press the keyboard combination Ctrl+e).

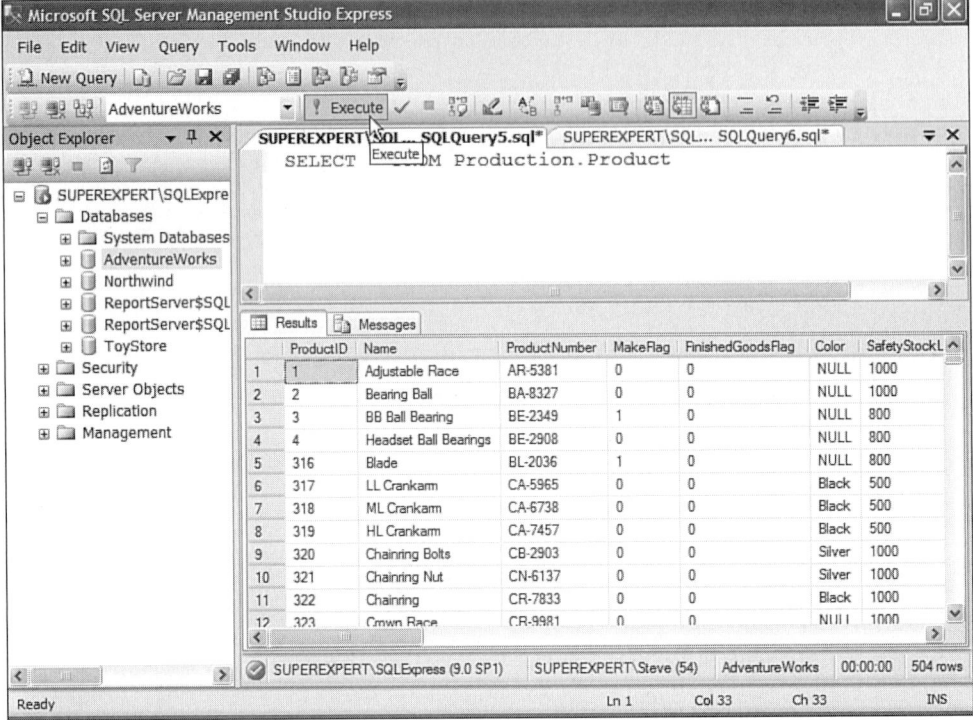

Figure 37   The Microsoft SQL Server Management Studio Express Query window.

Using the AdventureWorks Database

The AdventureWorks database is a sample database that contains sample data and is included with the full version of Microsoft SQL Server 2005. The SQL commands described in the following pages use the AdventureWorks database.

Microsoft SQL Server 2005 Express (the free edition of SQL Server included with Visual Web Developer) does not include the AdventureWorks sample database. However, you can download the AdventureWorks database from the Microsoft website. If you want to try out the SQL commands described in this section, I recommend that you grab this free download from the Microsoft site.

Servers, Databases, Schemas, and Tables

Information stored in a Microsoft SQL Server database is stored in a hierarchy of servers, databases, schemas, and tables. A Microsoft SQL Server server instance contains one or more databases that (optionally) contain one or more schemas, which contain one or more tables.

Typically, only one database server instance is installed on a computer. Furthermore, the name of a database server is typically the same as the name of the computer. So, if your computer is named MyLaptop and you have Microsoft SQL Server installed, the name of the database server will be MyLaptop. When you connect to the database server, you specify MyLaptop as the data source.

However, it is possible to have multiple instances of Microsoft SQL Server installed on the same machine. For example, on the laptop that I am typing on right now, I have two server instances installed. The default database server is a Microsoft SQL Server 2000 server instance (located at MyLaptop). In addition, my laptop contains a Microsoft SQL Server Express 2005 instance named SQLExpress (located at MyLaptop\SQLExpress).

Each database server instance can contain one or more databases. Typically, there is a one-to-one correspondence between applications and databases. For example, if I create a new web application called ToyStore, I also create a database named ToyStore.

Each database, in turn, can contain one or more schemas. Schemas are a new feature of Microsoft SQL Server 2005. Schemas provide you with a way to group related database objects together. For example, you can keep all of your database tables related to marketing in a schema named Marketing.

You are not required to use schemas explicitly when building a database. If you don't specify a schema when you create a database object, the object becomes part of a user's default schema (schemas are discussed later in more detail in the section titled "SQL Server Schemas").

Each schema, in turn, can contain one or more tables. The tables contain the actual information stored in the database. For example, the ToyStore database might contain a table named Products. Each row in the Products table might represent a particular product sold at the store.

Connecting to a Database

You connect to a database from an application by using a connection string. In a connection string, you specify the location of the database and the credentials required to connect to the database.

SQL Server 2005 gives you the option of supplying credentials in two ways. You can connect to a SQL database either by using Integrated Security or by using SQL Server authentication. When you use Integrated Security, you connect to a database by using your Microsoft Windows account. When you use SQL Server authentication, you connect to a database by supplying a username and password that you have defined in the database.

For example, the following connection string can be used to connect to a database named MyDatabase located on a server named MyLaptop. The connection string uses Integrated Security so that the user connects within the context of his or her Windows account.

```
Data Source=MyLaptop;Integrated Security=true;Initial Catalog=MyDatabase
```

So, what happens when you use this connection string in an ASP.NET page? Because an ASP.NET page executes in the security context of either the Windows ASPNET account (Windows XP) or the Windows NT AUTHORITY\NETWORK SERVICE account (Windows Server 2003), one of these two accounts, depending on the operating system, must have permission to access the database for the connection to be successful.

Here's a sample of a connection string that uses SQL Server authentication:

```
Data Source=MyLaptop;User Id=Steve;PWD=secret;Initial Catalog=MyDatabase
```

This connection string also can be used to connect to a database named MyDatabase on a server named MyLaptop. However, unlike the previous connection string, an explicit username and password are supplied in the connection string.

You should be aware that there exists a lot of variation in the way that developers write a connection string. There are many synonyms for the keywords that you can use in a connection string. For example, instead of using the keywords "Data Source," you can use the keyword "Server," and instead of using the keywords "Initial Catalog," you can use the keyword "Database." In the preceding connection strings, I am using the Microsoft canonical connection strings (but other forms still work).

Server Versus User Instance Database Connections

Connection strings become more complicated, and more interesting, when you use Microsoft SQL Server 2005 Express. Microsoft SQL Server Express supports two types of connections to a database: normal connections and user instance connections.

A *user instance* connection is a new type of connection introduced with SQL Server 2005 Express. When you use a user instance connection, you don't supply the name of a database in the connection string. Instead, you supply the file path to the database. When the connection is created, the database is attached to the SQL Server Express database server automatically. Furthermore, a copy of the database is created for the current user.

A user instance database connection looks like this:

```
Data Source=MyLaptop\SQLExpress; Integrated Security=true; AttachDBFileName=c:
\websites\website9\App_Data\MyDatabase.mdf; User Instance=true
```

Notice that the preceding connection string includes the "AttachDBFileName" keyword. This keyword is used to supply the file path to the SQL Server Express database file (MyDatabase.mdf). In the preceding connection string, a full path is given to the database file. When using a connection string in an ASP.NET page, you can use the special keyword "DataDirectory" to refer to the current website's App_Data folder like this:

```
Data Source=MyLaptop\SQLExpress; Integrated Security=true;
AttachDBFileName=¦DataDirectory¦MyDatabase.mdf; User Instance=true
```

Those are pipe characters (|) that appear on either side of the "DataDirectory" keyword.

Notice that the connection string also includes the special keyword "User Instance=true". When you use "AttachDBFileName" to attach a database to a SQL Express database server automatically, you should also use the "User Instance" keyword. This keyword causes a separate instance of the database to be created for the current user. This option enables a non-administrative user to attach a database (such as the NT AUTHORITY\NETWORK SERVICE account). Normally, only a database administrator can attach a database . Because normal users can auto-attach user instance databases, user instance databases are also called RANU (Run as Normal User) databases.

When you create a database in Visual Studio (or Visual Web Developer) by selecting **Website**, **Add New Item**, you are creating a database that you connect to by using a user instance connection. When you create a new database using Management Studio, on the other hand, you are creating a database that you connect to using a normal server connection.

SQL Server Security

To access or modify data from a Microsoft SQL Server database, you must have the right permissions. As mentioned earlier, Microsoft SQL Server supports two types of credentials: You can log in using your Windows account or you can log in using a custom username and password defined in SQL Server (SQL Server Express only supports Windows authentication).

A Microsoft SQL Server database server has one or more Logins. To access a Microsoft SQL Server database, you must supply the correct credentials for a particular Login configured for the database server. You create new Logins in Microsoft SQL Server Management Studio by expanding the Security folder, right-clicking the Logins folder, and selecting New Login.

A Login is defined at the level of the database server and not at the level of a particular database. In other words, the same Login can be used to connect to multiple databases on the same database server. You define the permissions of a particular Login for a particular database by mapping the Login to a database user. You specify a Login to user mapping by double-clicking the name of a **Login** (from the Logins folder) and selecting the **User Mappings** page (see Figure 38).

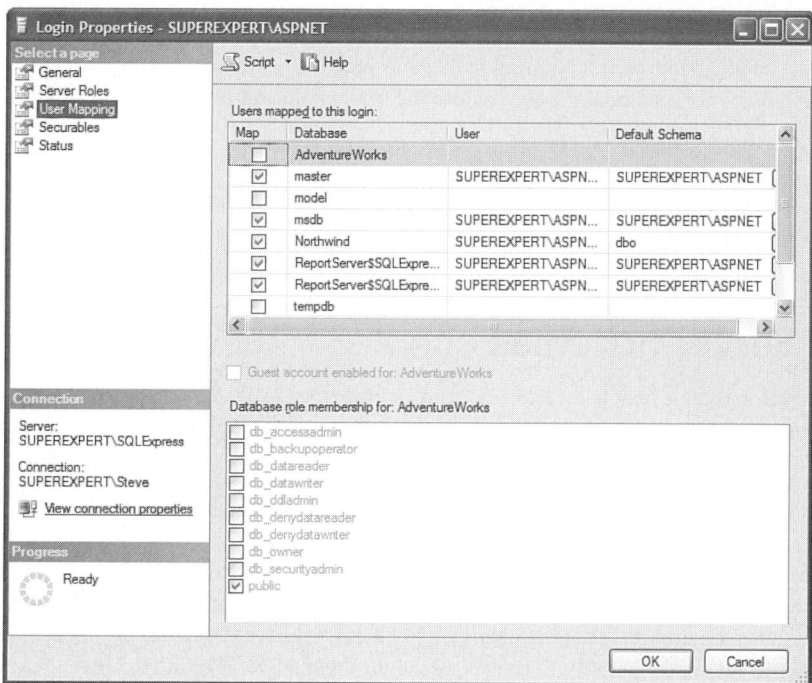

Figure 38   Mapping a Login to a database user.

Each database has its own set of users. You can view the set of users defined for a database by expanding a database folder, expanding the Security folder, and expanding the Users folder.

When you map a Login to a particular database, by default, a new database user is created with the same name as the Login. So, if you map the ASPNET Login to a database, by default a new database user named ASPNET is created.

You can define the permissions for a particular user for different database objects such as tables and stored procedures. For example, you might want to provide the ASPNET user permissions to select all the rows from a database table but not grant the ASPNET user permissions to insert or delete rows from the same table.

You specify user permissions on a table by right-clicking a database table in the Tables folder, selecting the **Properties** menu option, and selecting the **Permissions** page. Next, click the **Add** button to open the Select Users or Roles dialog box and then click the **Browse** button to select a particular user. Finally, you can click the **OK** button and select the permissions for the particular user.

Alternatively, you can set permissions by executing SQL commands (I find this method considerably faster). For example, to provide the GUEST account with SELECT permissions on the Products database table, you can execute the following SQL command:

```
GRANT SELECT on Products TO guest
```

You can remove this permission with the following statement:

```
REVOKE SELECT on Employees TO guest
```

The REVOKE command revokes a permission that was previously granted. If you want to explicitly deny a permission for a particular user, you use the DENY command like this:

```
DENY SELECT on Employees TO guest
```

You can also explicitly revoke a DENY command by executing a **REVOKE** command (the same REVOKE command as appears previously).

SQL Server Schemas

Database schemas are a new feature of Microsoft SQL Server 2005. When you create database objects, such as tables or stored procedures, you always create the new object within a particular schema.

If you look at the AdventureWorks database, the sample database included with Microsoft SQL Server, you'll notice that all the tables are grouped into schemas. If you launch Microsoft SQL Server Management Studio and expand the folder for the AdventureWorks database and you expand the folder for Tables, you'll see tables with names such as Production.Product, HumanResources.Employee, Person.Address, and Sales.Customer. The first part of each table name (the part before the period) represents a schema, and the second part (the part after the period) represents the actual table name.

Schemas are containers that you can use to group related database objects. For example, the AdventureWorks database groups all the database tables related to the Human Resources department in the HumanResources schema. This schema includes an Employee table, an EmployeeAddress table, and a JobCandidate table.

Within Microsoft Management Studio, you can create a new schema in a database by expanding the Security folder, right-clicking the folder labeled **Schemas**, and selecting the menu option **New Schema**. When you create a schema, you supply a name for the schema and you select a database user that owns the schema (see Figure 39).

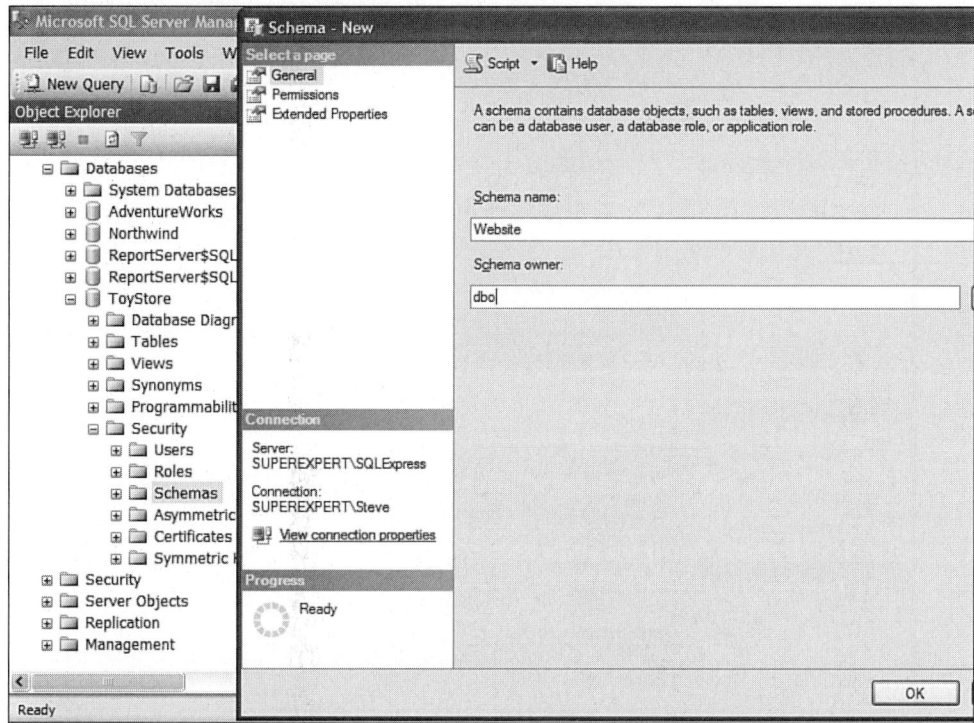

Figure 39   Creating a new database schema.

You also have the option of creating a schema by executing a SQL command. The following command creates a new schema named Website:

```
CREATE SCHEMA Website
```

If you don't specify a schema when you create a new table or stored procedure, the new table or stored procedure is added to your default schema. Typically, the default schema will be the dbo schema (database owner schema).

You can transfer objects between schemas. For example, if you want to transfer an existing table named Employees into the Website schema, then you can use the following SQL command:

```
ALTER SCHEMA Website TRANSFER dbo.Employees
```

Every user has a default schema. Unless you explicitly modify the default schema for a user, the default schema is the dbo schema. If you want to specify another default schema then expand the Security folder in a database, expand the Users folder, right-click a user, select the menu option **Properties**, and enter a new default schema (see Figure 40).

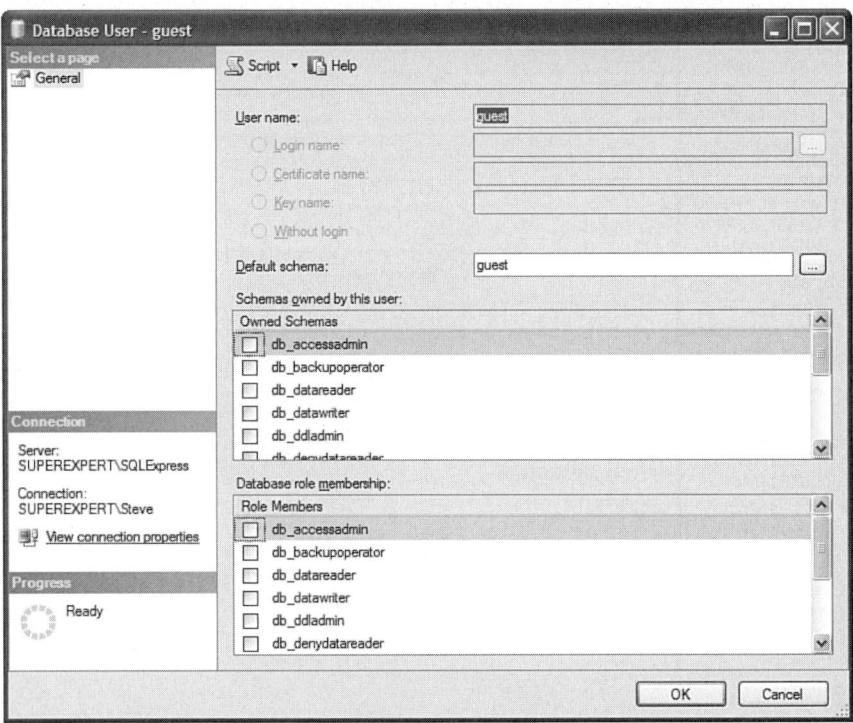

Figure 40   Specifying a user's default schema.

Creating New Database Tables

A schema contains one or more database tables. A database table contains the actual data stored in the database. A database table, as the name "table" suggests, consists of a set of columns and rows.

You define a database table by defining the types of columns that it contains. For example, if you want to create a database table that contains rows of product information, you might create a table that contains a ProductId column, a ProductPrice column, a ProductDescription column, and a ProductUnitsInStock column.

The easiest way to create a database table is to use either Visual Studio 2005 or Microsoft SQL Server 2005 Management Studio. Using either application, you can create a new database table by right-clicking the **Tables** folder located below a particular database (or data connection) and selecting **New Table** (see Figure 41).

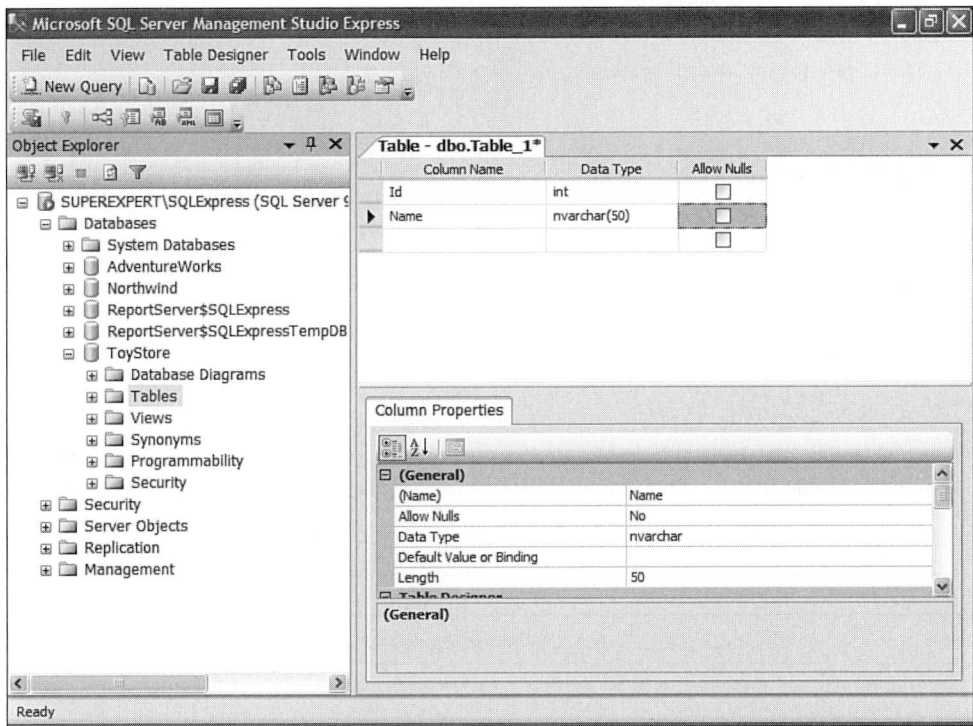

Figure 41   Creating a new database table.

As an alternative to creating a database table by using a visual tool, you can create a database table by issuing a SQL command: the CREATE TABLE command. For example, the following CREATE TABLE command could be used to create the Products database table:

```
CREATE TABLE Products
(
  ProductName NVarchar(50),
  ProductPrice Money,
  ProductDescription NVarchar(max)
)
```

Executing the preceding SQL statement creates a new database table that contains three columns: the ProductName, ProductPrice, and ProductDescription columns.

When you execute the CREATE TABLE command, the Products table is created in your default schema: the dbo schema. If you want to create the Products table in another schema, such as the Website schema, you would use a two-part table name when creating the table, like this:

```
CREATE TABLE Website.Products
(
    ProductName NVarchar(50),
    ProductPrice Money,
    ProductDescription NVarchar(max)
)
```

If you want to delete a database table after you create it, you can use the DROP TABLE command. The following command permanently removes the Products database table and all of its data from the default schema:

```
DROP TABLE Products
```

Be aware that if you drop a table, you never get its data back.

Database Column Types

When you create a database table, you must specify the data type of each of the database columns. The following table contains not a complete list, but a list of the most common data types supported by SQL Server 2005 (for a complete list, see the Microsoft SQL Server Books Online).

Data Type	Description
bit	Contains either 0 or 1. Useful for representing Boolean values.
datetime	Contains a date and time value. For example, the date and time that a record was created.
decimal	Contains a decimal number (a number such as 8.87978).
int	Contains an integer value between –2,147,483,648 and 2,147,483,647.
money	Represents a monetary amount between –922,337,203,685,477.5808 and 922,337,203,685,477.5807.
nvarchar	Contains a variable number of unicode characters up to 1,073,741,823 characters. Can be used for any type of text value, such as a person's first name or a person's resume.
varbinary	Contains a variable number of bytes up to 2,147,483,647 bytes. Useful for storing images.

Again, it's worth emphasizing that Microsoft SQL Server 2005 supports other data types, but 90% of the time, you'll find yourself using only the nvarchar, int, or datetime data types.

Identity Columns

A database table, optionally, can include an identity column. A table can have one, and at most one, identity column. An identity column is a column that automatically increments its value whenever a new row is added to a database table (identity columns are called Auto-Increment columns in Microsoft Access).

Just about every database table that I create includes an identity column. Identity columns are useful for uniquely identifying records. For example, if I want to delete a particular row from a database table, an identity column provides me with a way to uniquely identify the row that I want to delete.

When using Visual Studio or Management Studio, you can indicate that a numeric column (such as an int or decimal column) is an identity column by selecting the column and modifying the column properties (see Figure 42).

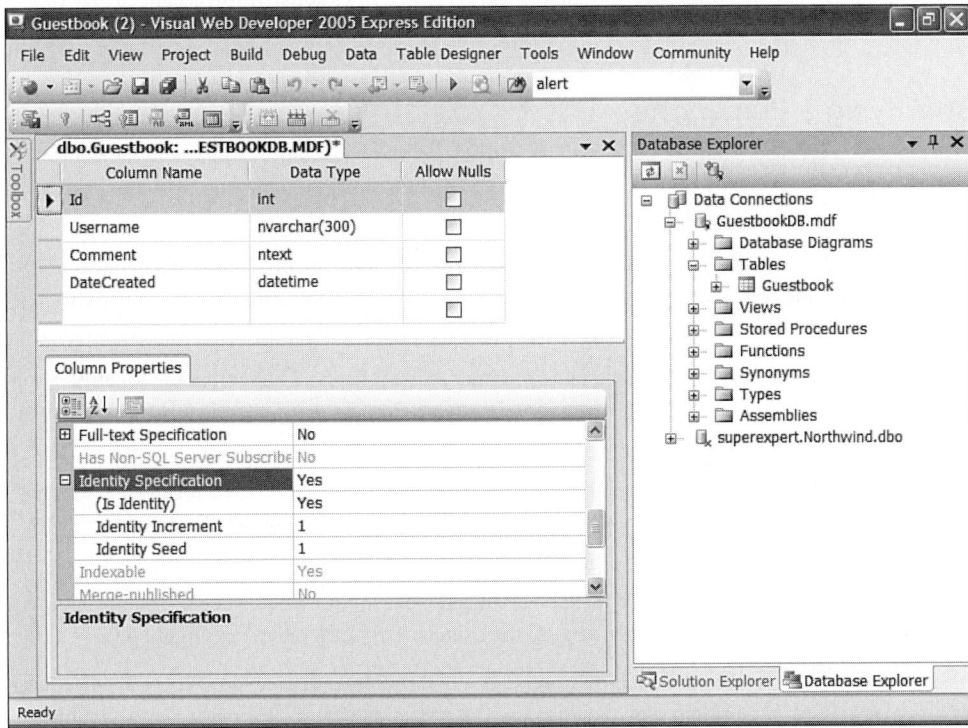

Figure 42   Specifying the identity column.

Alternatively, you can indicate that a particular column is an identity column when using the SQL CREATE TABLE statement like this:

```
CREATE TABLE Products
(
  ProductId Int Identity,
  ProductName NVarchar(50),
  ProductPrice Money,
  ProductDescription NVarchar(max)
)
```

After you execute this statement, a new table named Products is created. The Products table includes a column named ProductId. The ProductId column is an int column and an identity column. Every time you add a new row to this table, the value of the ProductId column is incremented automatically.

If you want to remove all the rows from a database table and reset the table's identity column, you can use the TRUNCATE TABLE command. The following statement truncates the Products database table:

```
TRUNCATE TABLE PRODUCTS
```

The TRUNCATE TABLE command is related to, but not the same as, the DROP TABLE command. The TRUNCATE TABLE command removes all the rows from a database table. However, the TRUNCATE TABLE command does not delete the table itself.

Specifying a Primary Key

Whenever you create a database table, you should also mark one or more columns in the database table as representing the primary key. The primary key for a database table uniquely identifies a particular row in the table.

For example, if you create an Employees database table that contains FirstName, LastName, and Phone columns, the primary key would consist of the FirstName and LastName columns. This would only work, of course, if no two employees could ever have the same first and last names.

Typically, I use an identity column as a table's primary key. Because I know that the identity column is guaranteed to be unique for each row in a table, I know that I can always use an identity column as a primary key.

Creating a primary key also creates a unique index for the database table. That means that queries using the columns defined as the primary key will execute faster than queries that use other columns in the database table.

When using Visual Studio 2005 or SQL Server Management Studio, you can select one or more columns and click the icon of a key to specify the primary key for a table (see Figure 43).

If you want to create a database table by executing a SQL command, and you want to specify that a particular column is a primary key, you can use the special keywords "Primary Key" like this:

```
CREATE TABLE Products
(
  ProductId Int Identity Primary Key,
  ProductName NVarchar(50),
  ProductPrice Money,
  ProductDescription NVarchar(max)
)
```

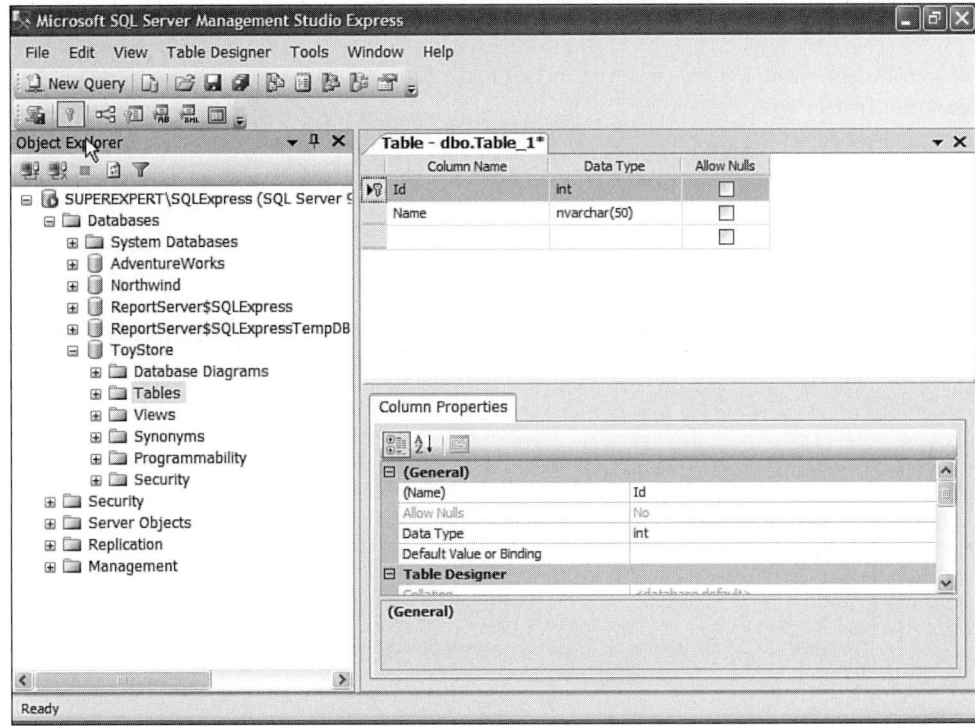

Figure 43   Specifying the primary key for a database table.

If you want to define a primary key that consists of multiple database columns, you can add a separate "Primary Key" clause like this:

```
CREATE TABLE Employees
(
  FirstName NVarchar(50),
  LastName NVarchar(50),
  Phone NVarchar(15),
  PRIMARY KEY (FirstName, LastName)
)
```

This statement creates a primary key that consists of the FirstName and LastName columns.

If you want to take advantage of the Visual Studio designer wizards when creating a SqlDataSource in an ASP.NET page, you should always specify a primary key for a table. The designer wizards won't function correctly unless you define a primary key for a table.

Selecting Rows from a Database Table

You retrieve information from a database by executing a SQL SELECT command. The SELECT command enables you to select rows from a database table. For example, the following SELECT command selects all the rows from the Product table located in the Production schema:

```
SELECT * FROM Production.Product
```

If you execute this statement from Management Studio, then you'll see the grid of results in Figure 44.

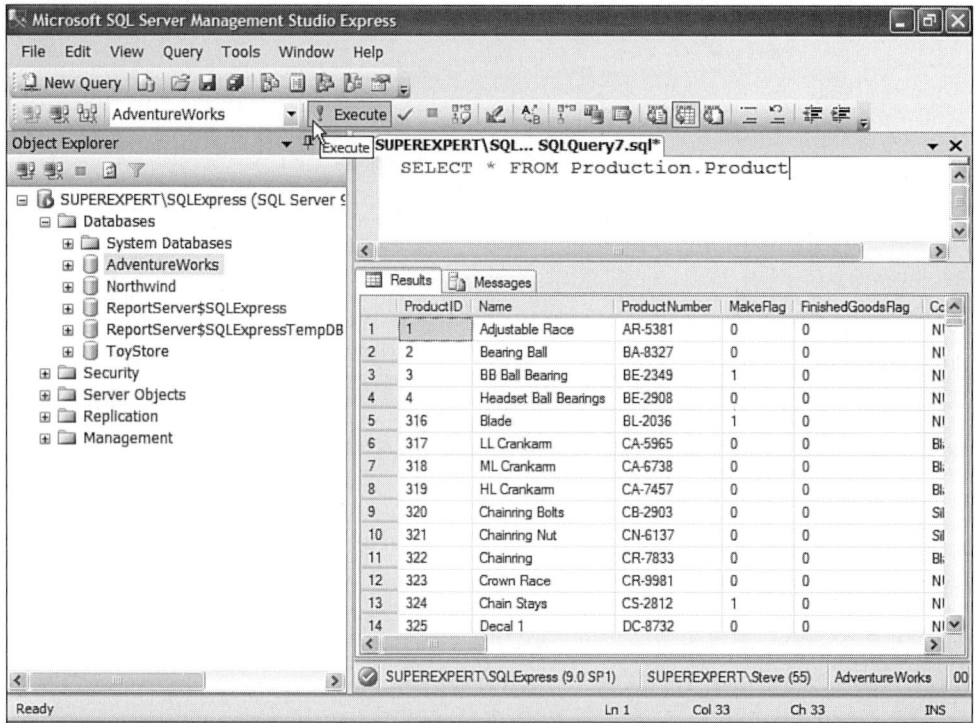

Figure 44   Displaying the results of a simple SELECT command.

The asterisk in the SELECT statement represents all the columns from the table. If you want to retrieve only particular columns, you can list the columns when executing the command like this:

```
SELECT ProductId, Name, ListPrice FROM Production.Product
```

This SELECT statement also retrieves all the rows from the Product table. However, the command retrieves only the values stored in the ProductId, Name, and ListPrice columns.

Specifying a WHERE Clause

Typically, you don't want to retrieve every row from a database table (a table might contain billions of rows). Instead, you want to retrieve only those rows that match a particular criterion. You use a WHERE clause with a SELECT statement to retrieve a subset of rows from a database table.

For example, the following SELECT command retrieves from the Product table only those products that cost more than $1,500 dollars:

```
SELECT Name, ListPrice
FROM Production.Product
WHERE ListPrice > 1500
```

You can use Boolean expressions within a WHERE clause to list multiple conditions. For example, the following command retrieves only red items that cost more than $1,500 dollars:

```
SELECT Name, ListPrice, Color
FROM Production.Product
WHERE ListPrice > 1500
AND Color = 'Red'
```

You can use AND, OR, and NOT within a WHERE clause to build up a WHERE clause with multiple conditions.

Retrieving the TOP Records

Another method of restricting the number of rows returned by a SELECT command is to include the TOP keyword in the query. The "Top" keyword enables you to retrieve the top so many records (or percent of records) from a table. For example, the following command retrieves no more than 10 records from the Products table:

```
SELECT TOP 10 Name, ListPrice
FROM Production.Product
```

In this case, you won't know exactly which set of 10 records will be returned. If you want to retrieve a particular set of records—for example, the first 10 records in order of price—you need to include an ORDER BY clause in your query (see the next section).

Specifying an ORDER BY Clause

Adding an ORDER BY clause to a SELECT command enables you to retrieve records from a database table arranged in a particular order. For example, if you want to show the records from the Products table in order from the least expensive to the most expensive products, you can use the following query:

```
SELECT Name, ListPrice
FROM Production.Product
ORDER BY ListPrice
```

This query returns rows from the Products table in ascending order. If you want to reverse the order of the rows returned by this query, you can use the "Desc" keyword in your ORDER BY clause like this:

```
SELECT Name, ListPrice
FROM Production.Product
ORDER BY ListPrice DESC
```

When you execute this query, the rows are arranged from most expensive to least expensive.

Using ORDER BY clauses is very useful when using the "Top" keyword since the ORDER BY clause enables you to specify the particular records returned. For example, the following query retrieves the last record entered into the Product table:

```
SELECT TOP 1 ProductId, Name, ListPrice
FROM Production.Product
ORDER BY ProductId DESC
```

This command orders the query results in order of the ProductId column. Because the last product added to the Product table will have the greatest ProductId, and the ORDER BY clause returns the row with the maximum ProductId, this query will return the last product added to the table.

Using Aggregate Functions

An aggregate function enables you to perform a calculation on the values of all the rows returned by a query for a particular column. For example, you can use an aggregate function to retrieve a sum of the values for every row, a count of the values for every row, or an average of the values for every row. You can also use an aggregate function to retrieve the minimum or maximum value of a column.

For example, the following query returns a count of the number of records contained in the Product database table:

```
SELECT COUNT(*) FROM Production.Product
```

Executing this query against the AdventureWorks database returns the value 504.

If you want to find the average list price of any red product, you can use the following query:

```
SELECT AVG(ListPrice)
FROM Production.Product
WHERE Color='Red'
```

It turns out that the average price for any red product in the AdventureWorks database is $1,409.95.

Joining Tables

Sometimes you need to retrieve related records from two tables. For example, the AdventureWorks database includes a table named Product, which contains product information, and a table named ProductReview, which contains customer reviews of the products in the Product table.

You can join the results of two tables together by using a `JOIN` operator. The most common type of `JOIN` operation is called an `INNER JOIN`. An `INNER JOIN` returns any row from one table that matches a row in a second table. Here's how you would use an `INNER JOIN` with the Product and ProductReview tables:

```
SELECT Product.Name, ProductReview.Comments
FROM Production.Product
INNER JOIN Production.ProductReview
  ON Product.ProductId = ProductReview.ProductId
```

Executing this `SELECT` command results in the set of records displayed in Figure 45. Rows from the Product table are matched to rows in the ProductReview table by using the value of the ProductId column.

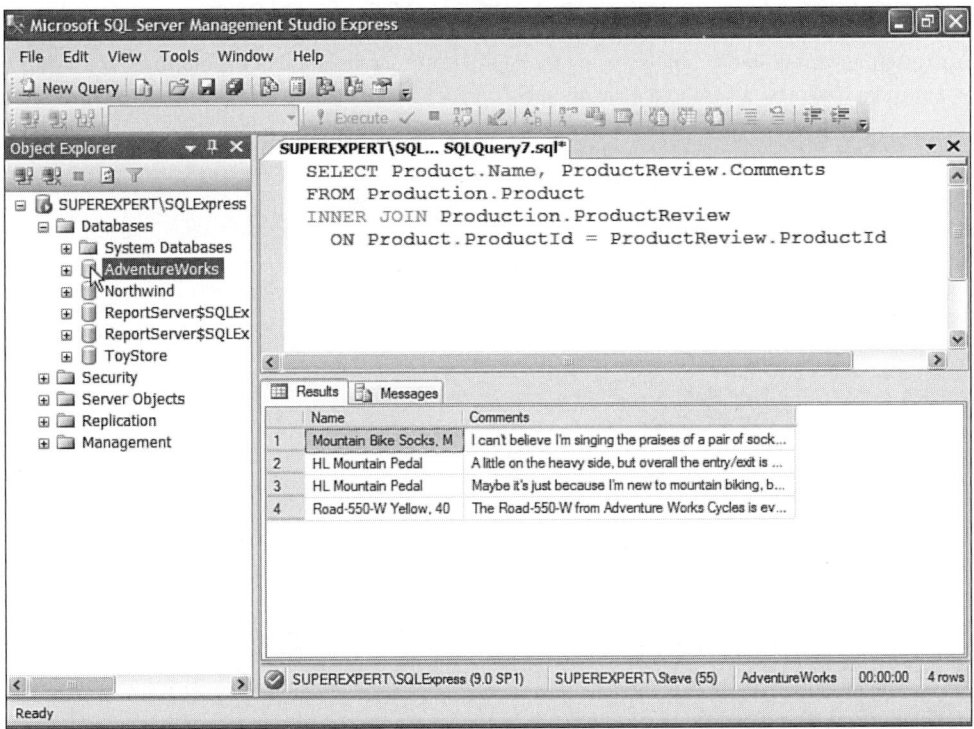

Figure 45   The results of an `INNER JOIN` operation.

There are types of `JOIN`s other than an `INNER JOIN`. An `INNER JOIN` will return only rows that share a common key across the two tables being joined. For example, when you execute the preceding command, only those products that have a product review are returned from the Product table. If you want to return all products regardless of whether the product has a review, you need to perform a `LEFT OUTER JOIN` like this:

```
SELECT Product.Name, ProductReview.Comments
FROM Production.Product
```

```
LEFT OUTER JOIN Production.ProductReview
  ON Product.ProductId = ProductReview.ProductId
```

When you execute this command, all the rows from the Product table are returned. If a product does not have a product review (which is true in the vast majority of cases), the value NULL is returned for the value of the Comments column.

A RIGHT OUTER JOIN returns all the rows from the second table being joined. However, it returns only those rows from the first table that match the second table.

Finally, a FULL OUTER JOIN returns all rows from both the first and second table. A row is returned from either table even when the row does not match a row from the other table.

Inserting Rows into a Database Table

You insert new rows into a table by using the SQL INSERT command. For example, the following command adds a new record to a database table named Address (located in the Person schema):

```
INSERT INTO Person.Address
(
     AddressLine1,
     AddressLine2,
     City,
     StateProvinceID,
     PostalCode
)
VALUES
(
     'Apt 36',
     '32 Main Street',
     'Seattle',
     1,
     '98144'
)
```

When you execute an INSERT command, you supply a list of table column names followed by a list of values for those columns.

Updating Existing Rows in a Database Table

You can modify existing rows in a database table by executing an UPDATE command. For example, the following command updates the one and only row in the Product table that has a ProductId of 3:

```
UPDATE Production.Product SET
  ListPrice = 12.33
WHERE ProductId = 3
```

This statement changes the ListPrice of the row with a ProductId of 3 to the value 12.33.

Be careful about the WHERE clause when you execute an UPDATE command. If you neglect to add the WHERE clause, then the UPDATE command updates every single row in the database table. If you have billions of records in a table, you could inadvertently modify billions of rows.

Deleting Existing Rows in a Database Table

You delete rows from a database table by using the DELETE command. For example, the following command deletes the row with an AddressId of 32522 from the Person.Address database table:

```
DELETE FROM Person.Address WHERE AddressId = 32522
```

Just like in the case of the UPDATE command, you need to be very careful to remember to include a WHERE clause when executing a DELETE command. The SQL language enables you to do incredibly stupid things very easily. If you neglect to add a WHERE clause to a DELETE command, you will delete every row from a database table.

If you really do want to delete every row from a database table, you should use the TRUNCATE TABLE command instead like this:

```
TRUNCATE TABLE Person.Address
```

An added benefit of using the TRUNCATE TABLE command is that it resets your identity column.

bonus ⊙ 2

An Introduction to the Microsoft ASP.NET Framework

In this section, you are provided with an overview of the Microsoft ASP.NET 2.0 framework. Because the best way to get familiar with the ASP.NET framework is to get your hands dirty by building an ASP.NET page, let's start by building a simple ASP.NET page.

NOTE

For information on installing ASP.NET, see the last section of this book.

If you are using Visual Web Developer or Visual Studio .NET, you first need to create a new website. Start Visual Web Developer and select the menu option **File**, **New Web Site**. The New Web Site dialog box appears (see Figure 46). Enter the folder where you want your new website to be created in the **Location** field and click the **OK** button.

After you create a new website, you can add an ASP.NET page to it. Select the menu option **Web Site**, **Add New Item**. Select **Web Form** and enter the value `FirstPage.aspx` in the Name field. Make sure that both the `Place Code in Separate File` and `Select Master Page` check boxes are unchecked, and click the **Add** button to create the new ASP.NET page (see Figure 47).

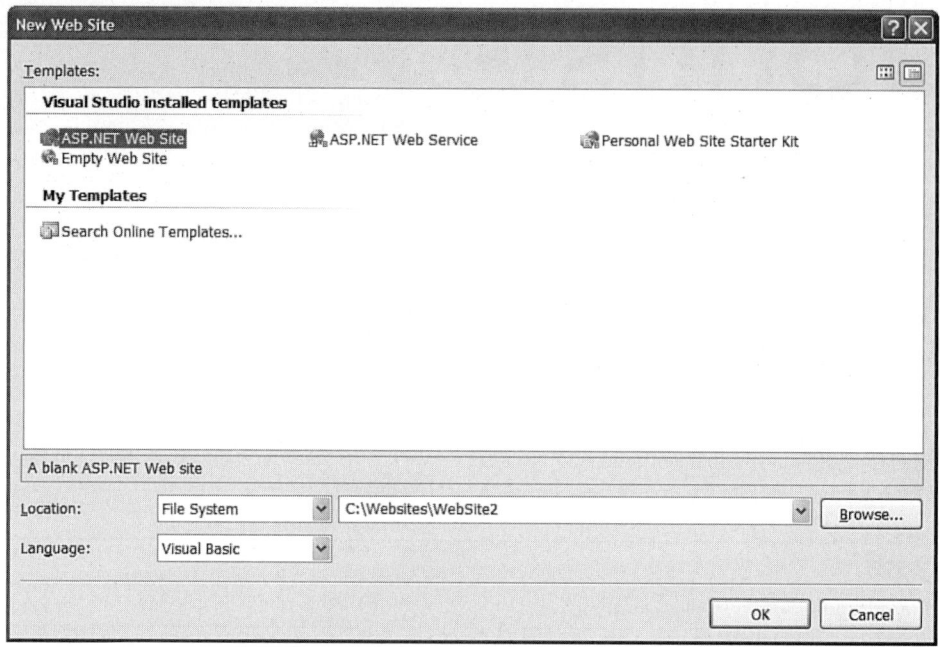

Figure 46   Creating a new website.

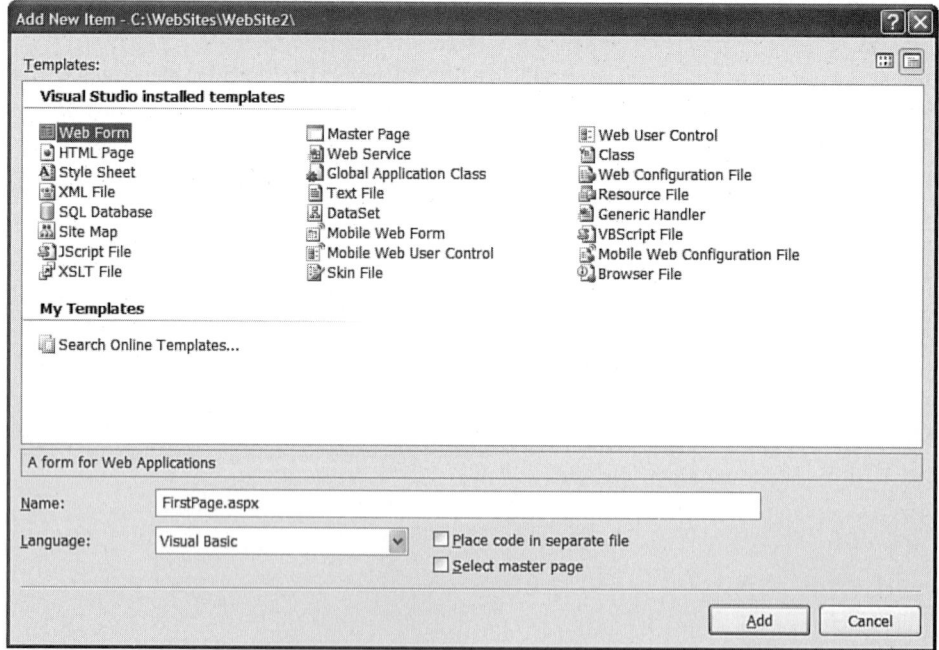

Figure 47   Adding a new ASP.NET page.

The code for the first ASP.NET page is contained in Listing 1.

Listing 1   FirstPage.aspx

```
<%@ Page Language="VB" %>
<!DOCTYPE html PUBLIC "-//W3C//DTD XHTML 1.0 Transitional//EN"
    "http://www.w3.org/TR/xhtml1/DTD/xhtml1-transitional.dtd">
<script runat="server">

    Sub Page_Load()
        lblServerTime.Text = DateTime.Now.ToString()
    End Sub

</script>
<html xmlns="http://www.w3.org/1999/xhtml" >
<head>
    <title>First Page</title>
</head>
<body>
    <form id="form1" runat="server">
    <div>

    Welcome to ASP.NET 2.0! The current date and time is:

    <asp:Label
        id="lblServerTime"
        Runat="server" />

    </div>
    </form>
</body>
</html>
```

The ASP.NET page in Listing 1 displays a brief message and the server's current date and time. You can view the page in Listing 1 in a browser by right-clicking the page and selecting **View in Browser** (see Figure 48).

The page in Listing 1 is an extremely simple page. However, it does illustrate the most common elements of an ASP.NET page. The page contains a directive, a code declaration block, and a page render block.

The first line in Listing 1 contains a directive. It looks like this:

```
<%@ Page Language="VB" %>
```

A directive always begins with the special characters <%@ and ends with the characters %>. Directives are used primarily to provide the compiler with the information it needs to compile the page.

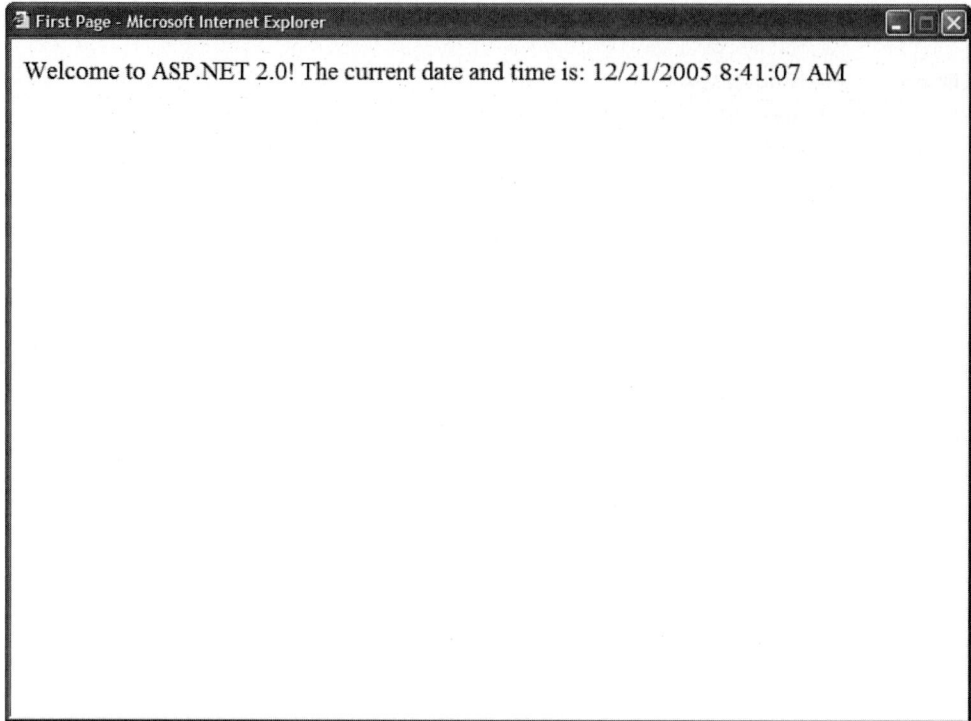

Figure 48   Viewing FirstPage.aspx in a browser.

For example, the directive in Listing 1 indicates that the code contained in the page is Visual Basic .NET (VB.NET) code. The page is compiled by the Visual Basic .NET compiler and not another compiler such as the C# compiler.

The next part of the page begins with the opening `<script runat="server">` tag and ends with the closing `</script>` tag. The `<script>` tag contains something called the code declaration block.

The code declaration block contains all the methods used in the page. It contains all the page's functions and subroutines. The code declaration block in Listing 1 includes a single subroutine named `Page_Load()`, which looks like this:

```
Sub Page_Load()
   lblServerTime.Text = DateTime.Now.ToString()
End Sub
```

This subroutine assigns the current date and time to the `Text` property of a `Label` control contained in the body of the page named `lblServerTime`.

The `Page_Load()` subroutine is an example of an event handler. This subroutine handles the `Page Load` event. Each and every time the page loads, the subroutine automatically executes and assigns the current date and time to the `Label` control.

The final part of the page is called the page render block. The page render block contains everything that is rendered to the browser. In Listing 1, the render block includes everything between the opening and closing <html> tags.

The majority of the page render block consists of everyday HTML. For example, the page contains the standard HTML <head> and <body> tags. In Listing 1, there are two special things contained in the page render block.

First, notice that the page contains a <form> tag that looks like this:

```
<form id="form1" runat="server">
```

This is an example of an ASP.NET control. Because the tag includes a runat="server" attribute, the tag represents an ASP.NET control that executes on the server.

ASP.NET pages are often called web form pages because they almost always contain a server-side form element.

The page render block also contains a Label control. The Label control is declared with the <asp:Label> tag. In Listing 1, the Label control is used to display the current date and time.

Controls are the heart of the ASP.NET framework. Most of your pain and effort when building ASP.NET pages is devoted to coaxing the ASP.NET controls to do what you want.

Controls are discussed in more detail shortly. However, first you need to understand the .NET framework.

NOTE

By default, ASP.NET pages are compatible with the XHTML 1.0 Transitional standard. You'll notice that the page in Listing 1 includes an XHTML 1.0 Transitional DOCTYPE. For details on how the ASP.NET framework complies with both XHTML and accessibility standards, see my article at the Microsoft MSDN website (msdn.Microsoft.com), titled "Building ASP.NET 2.0 Web Sites Using Web Standards."

ASP.NET and the .NET Framework

ASP.NET is part of the Microsoft .NET Framework. To build ASP.NET pages, you need to take advantage of the features of the .NET Framework. The .NET Framework consists of two parts: the Framework Class Library and the Common Language Runtime.

Understanding the Framework Class Library

The .NET Framework contains thousands of classes that you can use when building an application. The Framework Class Library was designed to make it easier to perform the most common programming tasks. Here are just a few examples of the classes in the framework:

- **File class**—Enables you to represent a file on your hard drive. You can use the File class to check whether a file exists, create a new file, delete a file, and perform many other file-related tasks.

- **Graphics class**—Enables you to work with different types of images such as GIF, PNG, BMP, and JPEG images. You can use the Graphics class to draw rectangles, arcs, ellipses, and other elements on an image.

- **Random class**—Enables you to generate a random number.

- **SmtpClient class**—Enables you to send email. You can use the SmtpClient class to send emails that contain attachments and HTML content.

These are only four examples of classes in the framework. The .NET framework contains almost 13,000 classes you can use when building applications.

You can view all the classes contained in the framework by opening the Microsoft .NET framework SDK documentation and expanding the Class Library node (see Figure 49). If you don't have the SDK documentation installed on your computer, see the last section of this book.

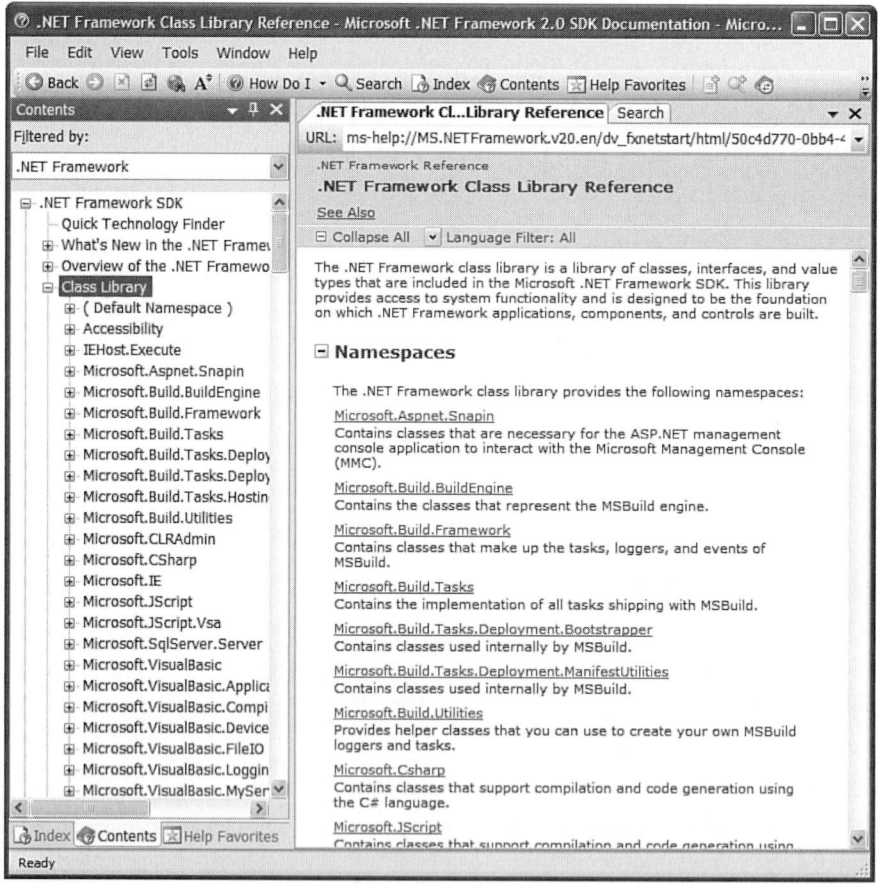

Figure 49   Opening the Microsoft .NET framework SDK documentation.

NOTE

The Microsoft .NET framework 2.0 includes 18,619 types, 12,909 classes, 401,759 public methods, 93,105 public properties, and 30,546 public events.

Each class in the framework can include properties, methods, and events. The properties, methods, and events exposed by a class are the members of a class. For example, here is a partial list of the members of the `SmtpClient` class:

- Properties
    - `Host`—The name or IP address of your email server
    - `Port`—The number of the port to use when sending an email message
- Methods
    - `Send`—Enables you to send an email message synchronously
    - `SendAsync`—Enables you to send an email message asynchronously
- Events
    - `SendCompleted`—Raised when an asynchronous send operation completes

If you know the members of a class, you know everything that you can do with a class. For example, the `SmtpClient` class includes two properties named `Host` and `Port`, which enable you to specify the email server and port to use when sending an email message.

The `SmtpClient` class also includes two methods you can use to send an email: `Send()` and `SendAsync()`. The Send method blocks further program execution until the send operation is completed. The `SendAsync()` method, on the other hand, sends the email asynchronously. Unlike the `Send()` method, the `SendAsync()` method does not wait to check whether the send operation was successful.

Finally, the `SmtpClient` class includes an event named `SendCompleted`, which is raised when an asynchronous send operation completes. You can create an event handler for the `SendCompleted` event that displays a message when the email has been successfully sent.

The page in Listing 2 sends an email by using the `SmtpClient` class and calling its `Send()` method.

Listing 2   SendMail.aspx

```
<%@ Page Language="VB" %>
<%@ Import Namespace="System.Net.Mail" %>
<!DOCTYPE html PUBLIC "-//W3C//DTD XHTML 1.0 Transitional//EN"
  "http://www.w3.org/TR/xhtml1/DTD/xhtml1-transitional.dtd">
<script runat="server">
```

continues

Listing 2   SendMail.aspx   *continued*

```
    Sub Page_Load()
        Dim client As New SmtpClient()
        client.Host = "localhost"
        client.Port = 25
        client.Send("steve@somewhere", "steve@superexpert.com", _
            "Let's eat lunch!", "Lunch at the Steak House?")
    End Sub

</script>
<html xmlns="http://www.w3.org/1999/xhtml" >
<head id="Head1" runat="server">
    <title>Send Mail</title>
</head>
<body>
    <form id="form1" runat="server">
    <div>

    Email sent!

    </div>
    </form>
</body>
</html>
```

The page in Listing 2 calls the `SmtpClient Send()` method to send the email. The first parameter is the from: address; the second parameter is the to: address; the third parameter is the subject; and the final parameter is the body of the email.

WARNING

The page in Listing 2 sends the email by using the local SMTP server. If your SMTP server is not enabled, you'll receive the following error: An existing connection was forcibly closed by the remote host. You can enable your local SMTP server by opening **Internet Information Services**, right-clicking **Default SMTP Virtual Server**, and selecting **Start**.

Understanding Namespaces

There are almost 13,000 classes in the .NET framework. This is an overwhelming number. If Microsoft simply jumbled all the classes together, you would never find anything. Fortunately, Microsoft divided the classes in the framework into separate *namespaces*.

A namespace is simply a category. For example, all the classes related to working with the file system are located in the `System.IO` namespace. All the classes for working a Microsoft SQL Server database are located in the `System.Data.SqlClient` namespace.

Before you can use a class in a page, you must indicate the namespace associated with the class. There are multiple ways of doing this.

First, you can fully qualify a class name with its namespace. For example, because the `File` class is contained in the `System.IO` namespace, you can use the following statement to check whether a file exists:

```
System.IO.File.Exists("SomeFile.txt")
```

Specifying a namespace each and every time you use a class can quickly become tedious (it involves a lot of typing). A second option is to import a namespace.

You can add an `<%@ Import %>` directive to a page to import a particular namespace. In Listing 2, we imported the `System.Net.Mail` namespace because the `SmtpClient` is part of this namespace. The page in Listing 2 includes the following directive near the very top of the page:

```
<%@ Import Namespace="System.Net.Mail" %>
```

After you import a particular namespace, you can use all the classes in that namespace without qualifying the class names.

Finally, if you discover that you are using a namespace in multiple pages in your application, you can configure all the pages in your application to recognize the namespace.

NOTE

A web configuration file is a special type of file that you can add to your application to configure your application. Be aware that the file is an XML file and, therefore, all the tags contained in the file are case sensitive. You can add a web configuration file to your application by selecting **Web Site**, **Add New Item** and selecting **Web Configuration File**.

If you add the web configuration file in Listing 3 to your application, you do not need to import the `System.Net.Mail` namespace in a page to use the classes from this namespace. For example, if you include the `Web.config` file in your project, you can remove the `<%@ Import %>` directive from the page in Listing 2.

Listing 3   Web.Config

```xml
<?xml version="1.0"?>
<configuration>
    <system.web>
      <pages>
        <namespaces>
          <add namespace="System.Net.Mail"/>
        </namespaces>
      </pages>
    </system.web>
</configuration>
```

You don't have to import every namespace. The ASP.NET framework gives you the most commonly used namespaces for free. These namespaces are as follows:

- `System`

- `System.Collections`

- `System.Collections.Specialized`

- `System.Configuration`

- `System.Text`

- `System.Text.RegularExpressions`

- `System.Web`

- `System.Web.Caching`

- `System.Web.SessionState`

- `System.Web.Security`

- `System.Web.Profile`

- `System.Web.UI`

- `System.Web.UI.WebControls`

- `System.Web.UI.WebControls.WebParts`

- `System.Web.UI.HTMLControls`

The default namespaces are listed inside the `pages` element in the root web configuration file located at the following path:

`\WINDOWS\Microsoft.NET\Framework\[version]\CONFIG\Web.Config`

Understanding Assemblies

An assembly is the actual `.dll` file on your hard drive where the classes in the .NET Framework are stored. For example, all the classes contained in the ASP.NET framework are located in an assembly named `System.Web.dll`.

More accurately, an assembly is the primary unit of deployment, security, and version control in the .NET Framework. Because an assembly can span multiple files, an assembly is often referred to as a "logical" dll.

NOTE

The .NET Framework (version 2.0) includes 51 assemblies.

There are two types of assemblies: private and shared. A private assembly can be used by only a single application. A shared assembly, on the other hand, can be used by all applications located on the same server.

Shared assemblies are located in the Global Assembly Cache (GAC). For example, the `System.Web.dll` assembly and all the other assemblies included with the .NET Framework are located in the Global Assembly Cache.

NOTE

The Global Assembly Cache is located physically in your computer's \WINDOWS\Assembly folder. There is a separate copy of every assembly in your \WINDOWS\Microsoft.NET\ Framework\v2.0.50727 folder. The first set of assemblies is used at runtime and the second set is used at compile time.

Before you can use a class contained in an assembly in your application, you must add a reference to the assembly. By default, an ASP.NET application references the most common assemblies contained in the Global Assembly Cache:

- `mscorlib.dll`

- `System.dll`

- `System.Configuration.dll`

- `System.Web.dll`

- `System.Data.dll`

- `System.Web.Services.dll`

- `System.Xml.dll`

- `System.Drawing.dll`

- `System.EnterpriseServices.dll`

- `System.Web.Mobile.dll`

To use any particular class in the .NET Framework, you must do two things. First, your application must reference the assembly that contains the class. Second, your application must import the namespace associated with the class.

In most cases, you won't worry about referencing the necessary assembly because the most common assemblies are referenced automatically. However, if you need to use a specialized assembly, you need to add a reference explicitly to the assembly. For example, if you need to interact with Active Directory by using the classes in the `System.DirectoryServices` namespace, you will need to add a reference to the `System.DirectoryServices.dll` assembly to your application.

Each class entry in the .NET Framework SDK documentation lists the assembly and namespace associated with the class. For example, if you look up the `MessageQueue` class in the documentation, you'll discover that this class is located in the `System.Messaging` namespace located in the `System.Messaging.dll` assembly.

If you are using Visual Web Developer, you can add a reference to an assembly explicitly by selecting the menu option **Web Site**, **Add Reference**, and selecting the name of the assembly that you need to reference. For example, adding a reference to the `System.Messaging.dll` assembly results in the web configuration file in Listing 4 being added to your application.

Listing 4   Web.Config

```
<?xml version="1.0"?>
<configuration>
<system.web>
  <compilation>
  <assemblies>
  <add
    assembly="System.Messaging, Version=2.0.0.0,
    Culture=neutral, PublicKeyToken=B03F5F7F11D50A3A" />
  </assemblies>
  </compilation>
</system.web>
</configuration>
```

If you prefer not to use Visual Web Developer, you can add the reference to the `System.Messaging.dll` assembly by creating the file in Listing 4 by hand.

Understanding the Common Language Runtime

The second part of the .NET Framework is the Common Language Runtime (CLR). The Common Language Runtime is responsible for executing your application code.

When you write an application for the .NET Framework with a language such as Visual Basic .NET or C#, your source code is never compiled directly into machine code. Instead, the Visual Basic or C# compiler converts your code into a special language named MSIL (Microsoft Intermediate Language).

MSIL looks very much like an object-oriented assembly language. However, unlike a typical assembly language, it is not CPU specific. MSIL is a low-level and platform-independent language.

When your application actually executes, the MSIL code is "just-in-time" compiled into machine code by the JITTER (the Just-In-Time compiler). Normally, your entire application is not compiled from MSIL into machine code. Instead, only the methods that are actually called during execution are compiled.

In reality, the .NET Framework understands only one language: MSIL. However, you can write applications using languages such as Visual Basic .NET and C# for the .NET Framework because the .NET Framework includes compilers for these languages that enable you to compile your code into MSIL.

You can write code for the .NET Framework using any one of dozens of different languages, including the following:

- Ada
- Apl
- Caml
- COBOL
- Eiffel
- Forth
- Fortran
- JavaScript

- Oberon
- PERL
- Pascal
- PHP
- Python
- RPG
- Scheme
- Small Talk

The vast majority of developers building ASP.NET applications write the applications in either Visual Basic .NET or C#. Many of the other .NET languages in the preceding list are academic experiments.

Once upon a time, if you wanted to become a developer, you concentrated on becoming proficient at a particular language. For example, you became a C++ programmer, a COBOL programmer, or a Visual Basic programmer.

When it comes to the .NET Framework, however, knowing a particular language is not particularly important. The choice of which language to use when building a .NET application is largely a preference choice. If you like case-sensitivity and curly braces, you should use the C# programming language. If you want to be lazy about casing and you don't like semicolons, write your code with Visual Basic .NET.

All the real action in the .NET Framework happens in the Framework Class Library. If you want to become a good programmer using Microsoft technologies, you need to learn how to use the methods, properties, and events of the 13,000 classes included in the Framework. From the point of view of the .NET Framework, it doesn't matter whether you are using these classes from a Visual Basic .NET or C# application.

Understanding ASP.NET Controls

ASP.NET controls are the heart of the ASP.NET framework. An ASP.NET control is a .NET class that executes on the server and renders certain content to the browser.

For example, in the first ASP.NET page created at the beginning of this introduction to ASP.NET 2.0, a `Label` control was used to display the current date and time. The ASP.NET framework includes more than 70 controls, which enable you to do everything from displaying a list of database records to displaying a randomly rotating banner advertisement.

In this section, you are provided with an overview of the controls included in the ASP.NET framework. You also learn how to handle events that are raised by controls and how to take advantage of View State.

Overview of ASP.NET Controls

The ASP.NET Framework (version 2.0) contains more than 70 controls. These controls can be divided into eight groups:

- **Standard controls**—The standard controls enable you to render standard form elements such as buttons, input fields, and labels.

- **Validation controls**—The validation controls enable you to validate form data before you submit the data to the server. For example, you can use a `RequiredFieldValidator` control to check whether a user entered a value for a required input field.

- **Rich controls**—The rich controls enable you to render things such as calendars, file upload buttons, rotating banner advertisements, and multistep wizards.

- **Data controls**—The data controls enable you to work with data such as database data. For example, you can use these controls to submit new records to a database table or display a list of database records.

- **Navigation controls**—The navigation controls enable you to display standard navigation elements such as menus, tree views, and bread crumb trails.

- **Login controls**—The login controls enable you to display login, change password, and registration forms.

- **Web Part controls**—The Web Part controls enable you to build personalizable portal applications.

- **HTML controls**—The HTML controls enable you to convert any HTML tag into a server-side control. We discuss this group of controls in the next section.

With the exception of the HTML controls, you declare and use all the ASP.NET controls in a page in exactly the same way. For example, if you want to display a text input field in a page, you can declare a `TextBox` control like this:

```
<asp:TextBox id="TextBox1" runat="Server" />
```

This control declaration looks like the declaration for an HTML tag. Remember, however, unlike an HTML tag, a control is a .NET class that executes on the server and not in the web browser.

When the `TextBox` control is rendered to the browser, it renders the following content:

```
<input name="TextBox1" type="text" id="TextBox1" />
```

The first part of the control declaration, the `asp:` prefix, indicates the namespace for the control. All the standard ASP.NET controls are contained in the `System.Web.UI.WebControls` namespace. The prefix `asp:` represents this namespace.

Next, the declaration contains the name of the control being declared. In this case, a `TextBox` control is being declared.

This declaration also includes an ID attribute. You use the ID to refer to the control in the page within your code. Every control must have a unique ID.

NOTE

You should always assign an ID attribute to every control even when you don't need to program against it. If you don't provide an ID attribute, certain features of the ASP.NET framework (such as two-way databinding) won't work.

The declaration also includes a `runat="Server"` attribute. This attribute marks the tag as representing a server-side control. If you neglect to include this attribute, the `TextBox` tag would be passed, without being executed, to the browser. The browser would simply ignore the tag.

Finally, notice that the tag ends with a forward slash. The forward slash is shorthand for creating a closing `</asp:TextBox>` tag. You can, if you prefer, declare the `TextBox` control like this:

```
<input name="TextBox1" type="text" id="TextBox1"></asp:TextBox>
```

In this case, the opening tag does not contain a forward slash and an explicit closing tag is included.

Understanding HTML Controls

You declare HTML controls in a different way than you declare standard ASP.NET controls. The ASP.NET framework enables you to take any HTML tag (real or imaginary) and add a `runat="server"` attribute to the tag. The `runat="server"` attribute converts the HTML tag into a server-side ASP.NET control.

For example, the page in Listing 5 contains a `<span>` tag, which has been converted into an ASP.NET control.

Listing 5   HtmlControls.aspx

```
<%@ Page Language="VB" %>
<!DOCTYPE html PUBLIC "-//W3C//DTD XHTML 1.0 Transitional//EN"
  "http://www.w3.org/TR/xhtml1/DTD/xhtml1-transitional.dtd">
<script runat="server">

    Sub Page_Load()
        spanNow.InnerText = DateTime.Now.ToString("T")
    End Sub

</script>
<html xmlns="http://www.w3.org/1999/xhtml" >
<head id="Head1" runat="server">
    <title>HTML Controls</title>
```

continues

Listing 5   HtmlControls.aspx *continued*

```
</head>
<body>
    <form id="form1" runat="server">
    <div>

    At the tone, the time will be:
    <span id="spanNow" runat="server" />

    </div>
    </form>
</body>
</html>
```

Notice that the <span> tag in Listing 5 looks just like a normal HTML <span> tag except for the addition of the runat="server" attribute.

Because the <span> tag in Listing 5 is a server-side HTML control, you can program against it. In Listing 5, the current date and time are assigned to the <span> tag in the Page_Load() method.

The HTML controls are included in the ASP.NET framework to make it easier to convert existing HTML pages to use the ASP.NET framework. I rarely use the HTML controls because, in general, the standard ASP.NET controls provide all the same functionality and more.

Understanding and Handling Control Events

The majority of the ASP.NET controls support one or more events. For example, the ASP.NET Button control supports the Click event. The Click event is raised on the server after you click the button rendered by the Button control in the browser.

The page in Listing 6 illustrates how you can write code that executes when a user clicks the button rendered by the Button control (in other words, it illustrates how you can create a Click event handler).

Listing 6   ShowButtonClick.aspx

```
<%@ Page Language="VB" %>
<!DOCTYPE html PUBLIC "-//W3C//DTD XHTML 1.0 Transitional//EN"
  "http://www.w3.org/TR/xhtml1/DTD/xhtml1-transitional.dtd">
<script runat="server">

    Sub btnSubmit_Click(ByVal sender As Object, ByVal e As EventArgs)
        Label1.Text = "Thanks!"
    End Sub
</script>
```

```
<html xmlns="http://www.w3.org/1999/xhtml" >
<head id="Head1" runat="server">
    <title>Show Button Click</title>
</head>
<body>
    <form id="form1" runat="server">
    <div>

    <asp:Button
        id="btnSubmit"
        Text="Click Here"
        OnClick="btnSubmit_Click"
        Runat="server" />

    <br /><br />

    <asp:Label
        id="Label1"
        Runat="server" />

    </div>
    </form>
</body>
    </html>
```

Notice that the Button control in Listing 6 includes an OnClick attribute. This attribute points to a subroutine named btnSubmit_Click(). The btnSubmit_Click() subroutine is the handler for the Button Click event. This subroutine executes whenever you click the button (see Figure 50).

You can add an event handler automatically to a control in multiple ways when using Visual Web Developer. In Source view, add a handler by selecting a control from the top-left drop-down list and selecting an event from the top-right drop-down list. The event handler code is added to the page automatically (see Figure 51).

In Design view, you can double-click a control to add a handler for the control's default event. Double-clicking a control switches you to Source view and adds the event handler.

Figure 50   Raising a Click event.

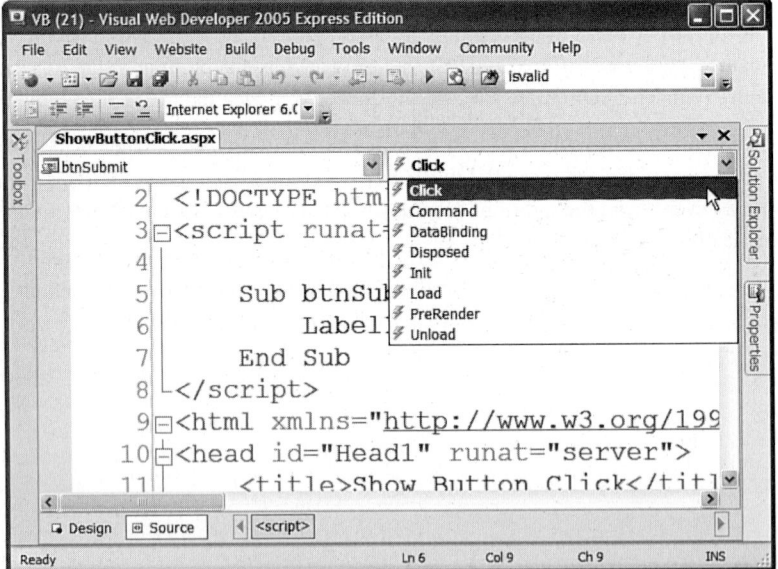

Figure 51   Adding an event handler from Source view.

Finally, from Design view, after selecting a control on the designer surface, you can add an event handler from the Properties window by clicking the Events button (the lightning bolt) and double-clicking next to the name of any of the events (see Figure 52).

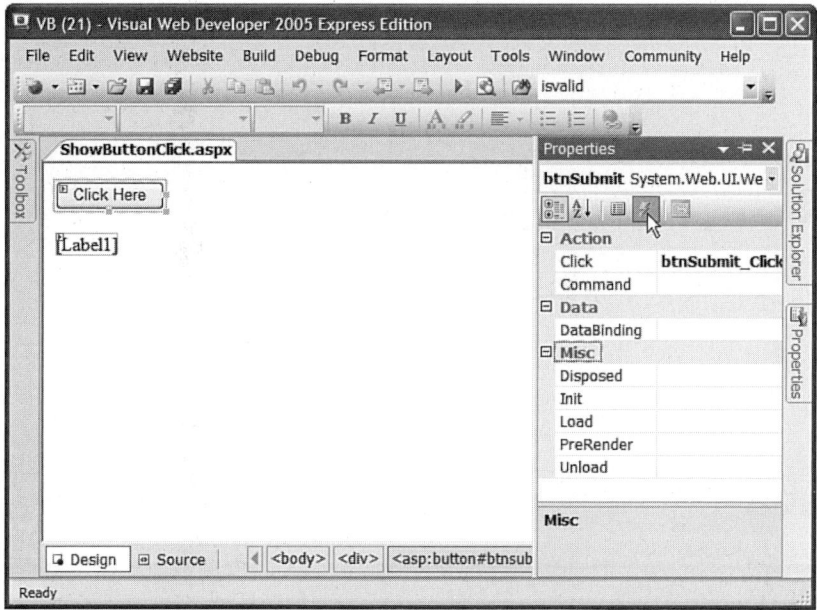

Figure 52   Adding an event handler from the Properties window.

It is important to understand that all ASP.NET control events happen on the server. For example, the Click event is not raised when you actually click a button. The Click event is not raised until the page containing the Button control is posted back to the server.

The ASP.NET framework is a server-side web application framework. The .NET Framework code that you write executes on the server and not within the web browser. From the perspective of ASP.NET, nothing happens until the page is posted back to the server and can execute within the context of the .NET Framework.

Notice that two parameters are passed to the btnSubmit_Click() handler in Listing 6. All event handlers for ASP.NET controls have the same general signature.

The first parameter, the object parameter named sender, represents the control that raised the event. In other words, it represents the Button control that you clicked.

You can wire multiple controls in a page to the same event handler and use this first parameter to determine the particular control that raised the event. For example, the page in Listing 7 includes two Button controls. When you click either Button control, the text displayed by the Button control is updated (see Figure 53).

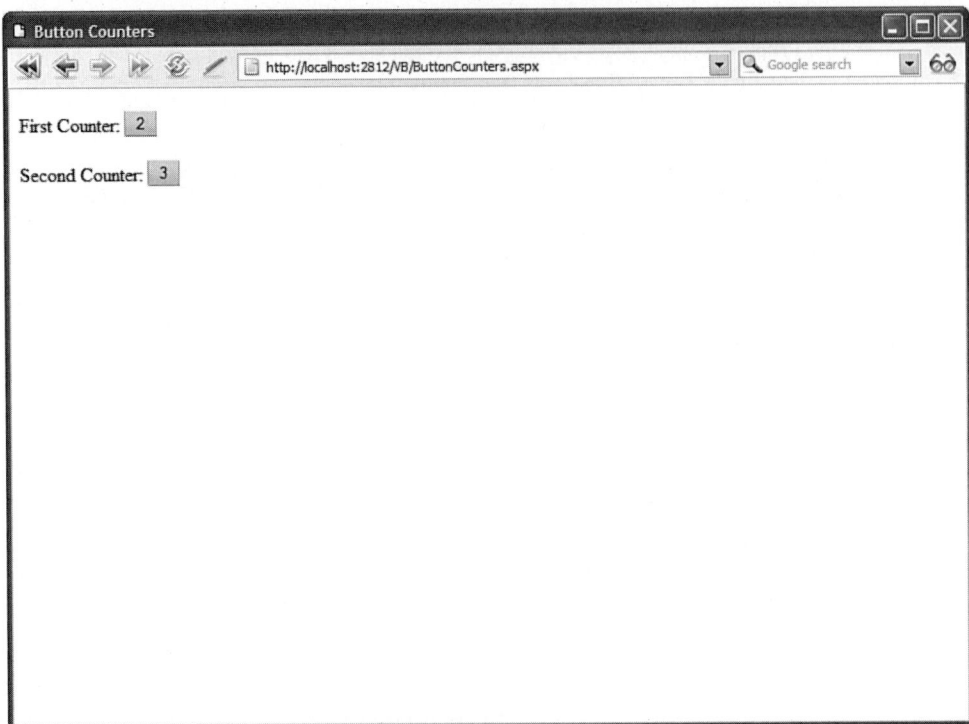

Figure 53   Handling two Button controls with one event handler.

Listing 7   ButtonCounters.aspx

```
<%@ Page Language="VB" %>
<!DOCTYPE html PUBLIC "-//W3C//DTD XHTML 1.0 Transitional//EN"
 "http://www.w3.org/TR/xhtml1/DTD/xhtml1-transitional.dtd">
<script runat="server">

    Sub Button_Click(ByVal sender As Object, ByVal e As EventArgs)
        Dim btn As Button = CType(sender, Button)
        btn.Text = (Int32.Parse(btn.Text) + 1).ToString()
    End Sub
</script>
<html xmlns="http://www.w3.org/1999/xhtml" >
<head id="Head1" runat="server">
    <title>Button Counters</title>
```

```
</head>
<body>
    <form id="form1" runat="server">
    <div>

    First Counter:
    <asp:Button
        id="Button1"
        Text="0"
        OnClick="Button_Click"
        Runat="server" />

    <br /><br />

    Second Counter:
    <asp:Button
        id="Button2"
        Text="0"
        OnClick="Button_Click"
        Runat="server" />

    </div>
    </form>
</body>
    </html>
```

The second parameter passed to the Click event handler, the EventArgs parameter named e, represents any additional event information associated with the event. No additional event information is associated with clicking a button, so this second parameter does not represent anything useful in either Listing 6 or Listing 7.

When you click an ImageButton control instead of a Button control, on the other hand, additional event information is passed to the event handler. When you click an ImageButton control, the X and Y coordinates of where you clicked are passed to the handler.

The page in Listing 8 contains an ImageButton control that displays a picture. When you click the picture, the X and Y coordinates of the spot you clicked are displayed in a Label control (see Figure 54).

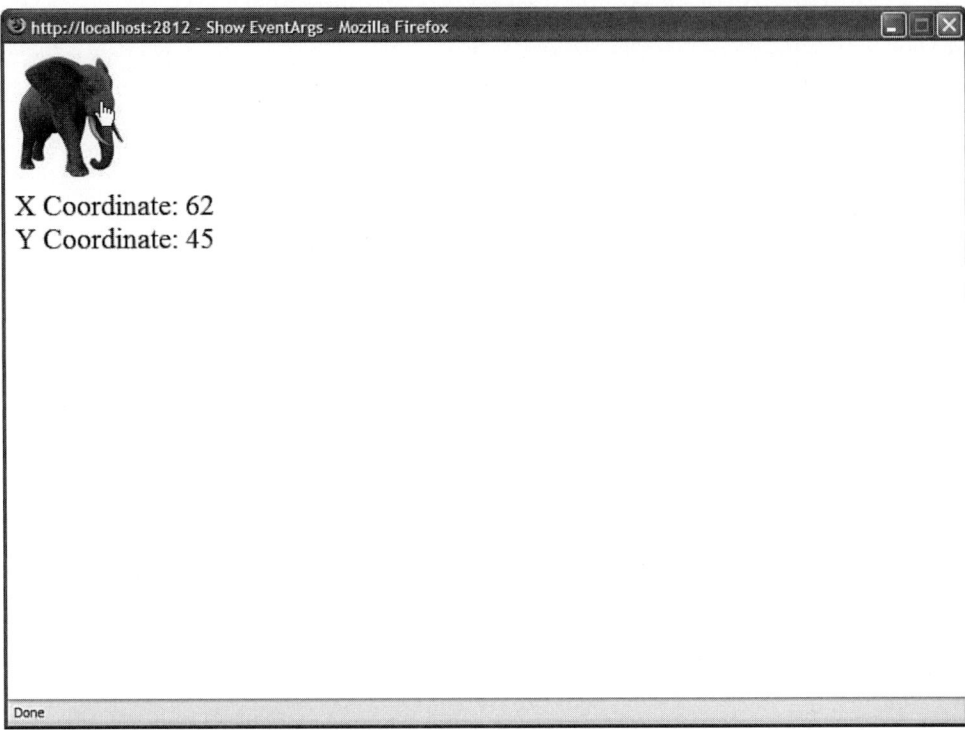

Figure 54   Clicking an ImageButton.

Listing 8   ShowEventArgs.aspx

```
<%@ Page Language="VB" %>
<!DOCTYPE html PUBLIC "-//W3C//DTD XHTML 1.0 Transitional//EN"
    "http://www.w3.org/TR/xhtml1/DTD/xhtml1-transitional.dtd">
<script runat="server">

    Sub btnElephant_Click(ByVal sender As Object, ByVal e As ImageClickEventArgs)
        lblX.Text = e.X.ToString()
        lblY.Text = e.Y.ToString()
    End Sub
</script>
<html xmlns="http://www.w3.org/1999/xhtml" >
<head id="Head1" runat="server">
    <title>Show EventArgs</title>
</head>
<body>
```

```
<form id="form1" runat="server">
<div>

<asp:ImageButton
    id="btnElephant"
    ImageUrl="Elephant.jpg"
    OnClick="btnElephant_Click"
    Runat="server" />

<br />
X Coordinate:
<asp:Label
    id="lblX"
    Runat="server" />
<br />
Y Coordinate:
<asp:Label
    id="lblY"
    Runat="server" />

</div>
</form>
</body>
</html>
```

Notice that the second parameter passed to the `btnElephant_Click()` method is an `ImageClickEventArgs` parameter. Whenever the second parameter is not the default `EventArgs` parameter, you know that additional event information is being passed to the handler.

Understanding View State

The HTTP protocol, the fundamental protocol of the World Wide Web, is a stateless protocol. Each time you request a web page from a website, from the website's perspective, you are a completely new person.

The ASP.NET framework, however, manages to transcend this limitation of the HTTP protocol. For example, if you assign a value to a `Label` control's `Text` property, the `Label` control retains this value across multiple page requests.

Consider the page in Listing 9. This page contains a `Button` control and a `Label` control. Each time you click the `Button` control, the value displayed by the `Label` control is incremented by 1 (see Figure 55). How does the `Label` control preserve its value across postbacks to the web server?

Figure 55   Preserving state between postbacks.

Listing 9   ShowViewState.aspx

```
<%@ Page Language="VB" %>
<!DOCTYPE html PUBLIC "-//W3C//DTD XHTML 1.0 Transitional//EN"
    "http://www.w3.org/TR/xhtml1/DTD/xhtml1-transitional.dtd">
<script runat="server">

    Sub btnAdd_Click(ByVal sender As Object, ByVal e As EventArgs)
        lblCounter.Text = (Int32.Parse(lblCounter.Text) + 1).ToString()
    End Sub
</script>
<html xmlns="http://www.w3.org/1999/xhtml" >
<head id="Head1" runat="server">
    <title>Show View State</title>
</head>
<body>
    <form id="form1" runat="server">
```

```
    <div>

    <asp:Button
        id="btnAdd"
        Text="Add"
        OnClick="btnAdd_Click"
        Runat="server" />

    <asp:Label
        id="lblCounter"
        Text="0"
        Runat="server" />

    </div>
    </form>
</body>
    </html>
```

The ASP.NET framework uses a trick called View State. If you open the page in Listing 9 in your browser and select View Source, you'll notice that the page includes a hidden form field named __VIEWSTATE that looks like this:

```
<input type="hidden" name="__VIEWSTATE" id="
  __VIEWSTATE" value="/wEPDwUKLTc2ODE1OTYxNw9kFgICBA9kFgIC
  Aw8PFgIeBFRleHQFATFkZGT3tMnThg9KZpGak55p367vfInj1w==" />
```

This hidden form field contains the value of the Label control's Text property (and the values of any other control properties that are stored in View State). When the page is posted back to the server, the ASP.NET framework rips apart this string and re-creates the values of all the properties stored in View State. In this way, the ASP.NET framework preserves the state of control properties across postbacks to the web server.

By default, View State is enabled for every control in the ASP.NET framework. If you change the background color of a Calendar control, the new background color is remembered across post-backs. If you change the selected item in a DropDownList, the selected item is remembered across postbacks. The values of these properties are automatically stored in View State.

View State is a good thing, but sometimes it can be too much of a good thing. The __VIEWSTATE hidden form field can become very large. Stuffing too much data into View State can slow down the rendering of a page because the contents of the hidden field must be pushed back and forth between the web server and web browser.

You can determine how much View State each control contained in a page is consuming by enabling tracing for a page (see Figure 56). The page in Listing 10 includes a Trace="true" attribute in its <%@ Page %> directive, which enables tracing.

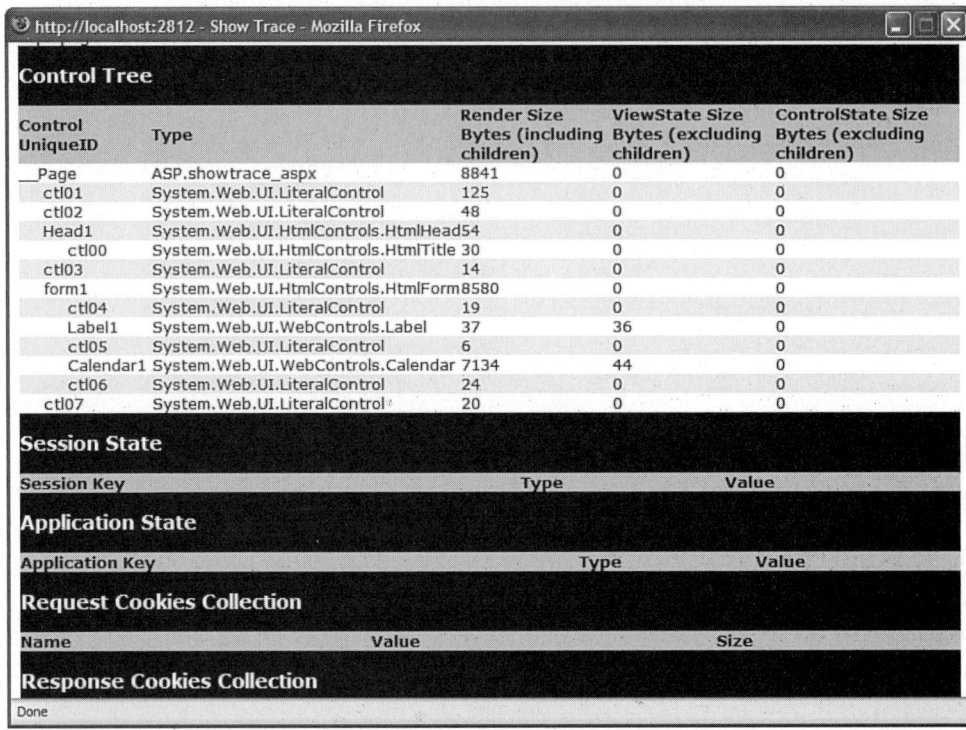

Figure 56   Viewing View State size for each control.

Listing 10   ShowTrace.aspx

```
<%@ Page Language="VB" Trace="true" %>
<!DOCTYPE html PUBLIC "-//W3C//DTD XHTML 1.0 Transitional//EN"
    "http://www.w3.org/TR/xhtml1/DTD/xhtml1-transitional.dtd">
<script runat="server">

    Sub Page_Load()
        Label1.Text = "Hello World!"
        Calendar1.TodaysDate = DateTime.Now
    End Sub

</script>
<html xmlns="http://www.w3.org/1999/xhtml" >
<head id="Head1" runat="server">
    <title>Show Trace</title>
</head>
<body>
    <form id="form1" runat="server">
    <div>
```

```
<asp:Label
    id="Label1"
    Runat="server" />
<asp:Calendar
    id="Calendar1"
    TodayDayStyle-BackColor="Yellow"
    Runat="server" />

</div>
</form>
</body>
</html>
```

When you open the page in Listing 10, additional information about the page is appended to the bottom of the page. The Control Tree section displays the amount of View State used by each ASP.NET control contained in the page.

Every ASP.NET control includes a property named `EnableViewState`. If you set this property to the value `False`, View State is disabled for the control. In that case, the values of the control properties are not remembered across postbacks to the server.

For example, the page in Listing 11 contains two `Label` controls and a `Button` control. The first label has View State disabled and the second label has View State enabled. When you click the button, only the value of the second `Label` control is incremented past 1.

Listing 11   DisableViewState.aspx

```
<%@ Page Language="VB" %>
<!DOCTYPE html PUBLIC "-//W3C//DTD XHTML 1.0 Transitional//EN"
    "http://www.w3.org/TR/xhtml1/DTD/xhtml1-transitional.dtd">
<script runat="server">

    Sub btnAdd_Click(ByVal sender As Object, ByVal e As EventArgs)
        Label1.Text = (Int32.Parse(Label1.Text) + 1).ToString()
        Label2.Text = (Int32.Parse(Label2.Text) + 1).ToString()
    End Sub
</script>
<html xmlns="http://www.w3.org/1999/xhtml" >
<head id="Head1" runat="server">
    <title>Disable View State</title>
</head>
<body>
    <form id="form1" runat="server">
    <div>

    Label 1:
```

continues

Listing 11   DisableViewState.aspx   *continued*

```
<asp:Label
    id="Label1"
    EnableViewState="false"
    Text="0"
    Runat="server" />

<br />

Label 2:
<asp:Label
    id="Label2"
    Text="0"
    Runat="server" />

<br /><br />

<asp:Button
    id="btnAdd"
    Text="Add"
    OnClick="btnAdd_Click"
    Runat="server" />

</div>
</form>
</body>
</html>
```

Sometimes, you might want to disable View State even when you aren't concerned with the size of the __VIEWSTATE hidden form field. For example, if you are using a Label control to display a form validation error message, you might want to start from scratch each time the page is submitted. In that case, simply disable View State for the Label control.

NOTE

The ASP.NET framework version 2.0 includes a new feature called Control State. Control State is similar to View State except that it is used to preserve only critical state information. For example, the GridView control uses Control State to store the selected row. Even if you disable View State, the GridView control remembers which row is selected.

Understanding ASP.NET Pages

This section examines ASP.NET pages in more detail. You learn about dynamic compilation and code-behind files. We also discuss the events supported by the Page class.

Understanding Dynamic Compilation

Strangely enough, when you create an ASP.NET page, you are actually creating the source code for a .NET class. You are creating a new instance of the System.Web.UI.Page class. The entire contents of an ASP.NET page, including all script and HTML content, are compiled into a .NET class.

When you request an ASP.NET page, the ASP.NET framework checks for a .NET class that corresponds to the page. If a corresponding class does not exist, the framework automatically compiles the page into a new class and stores the compiled class (the assembly) in the Temporary ASP.NET Files folder located at the following path:

```
\WINDOWS\Microsoft.NET\Framework\[version]\Temporary ASP.NET Files
```

The next time anyone requests the same page in the future, the page is not compiled again. The previously compiled class is executed, and the results are returned to the browser.

Even if you unplug your web server, move to Borneo for three years, and start up your web server again, the next time someone requests the same page, the page does not need to be recompiled. The compiled class is preserved in the Temporary ASP.NET Files folder until the source code for your application is modified.

When the class is added to the Temporary ASP.NET Files folder, a file dependency is created between the class and the original ASP.NET page. If the ASP.NET page is modified in any way, the corresponding .NET class is automatically deleted. The next time someone requests the page, the framework automatically compiles the modified page source into a new .NET class.

This process is called *dynamic compilation*. Dynamic compilation enables ASP.NET applications to support thousands of simultaneous users. Unlike an ASP Classic page, for example, an ASP.NET page does not need to be parsed and compiled each and every time it is requested. An ASP.NET page is compiled only when an application is modified.

NOTE

You can precompile an entire ASP.NET application by using the aspnet_compiler.exe command-line tool. If you precompile an application, users don't experience the compilation delay resulting from the first page request.

Understanding Control Trees

In the previous section, you learned that an ASP.NET page is really the source code for a .NET class. Alternatively, you can think of an ASP.NET page as a bag of controls. More accurately, because some controls might contain child controls, you can think of an ASP.NET page as a control tree.

For example, the page in Listing 12 contains a DropDownList control and a Button control. Furthermore, because the <%@ Page %> directive has the Trace="true" attribute, tracing is enabled for the page.

Listing 12   ShowControlTree.aspx

```
<%@ Page Language="VB" Trace="true" %>
<!DOCTYPE html PUBLIC "-//W3C//DTD XHTML 1.0 Transitional//EN"
 "http://www.w3.org/TR/xhtml1/DTD/xhtml1-transitional.dtd">
<html xmlns="http://www.w3.org/1999/xhtml" >
<head id="Head1" runat="server">
    <title>Show Control Tree</title>
</head>
<body>
    <form id="form1" runat="server">
    <div>

    <asp:DropDownList
        id="DropDownList1"
        Runat="server">
        <asp:ListItem Text="Oranges" />
        <asp:ListItem Text="Apples" />
    </asp:DropDownList>

    <asp:Button
        id="Button1"
        Text="Submit"
        Runat="server" />

    </div>
    </form>
</body>
</html>
```

When you open the page in Listing 12 in your browser, you can see the control tree for the page appended to the bottom of the page. It looks like this:

```
__Page ASP.showcontroltree_aspx
    ctl02 System.Web.UI.LiteralControl
    ctl00 System.Web.UI.HtmlControls.HtmlHead
        ctl01 System.Web.UI.HtmlControls.HtmlTitle
    ctl03 System.Web.UI.LiteralControl
    form1 System.Web.UI.HtmlControls.HtmlForm
        ctl04 System.Web.UI.LiteralControl
        DropDownList1 System.Web.UI.WebControls.DropDownList
        ctl05 System.Web.UI.LiteralControl
        Button1 System.Web.UI.WebControls.Button
        ctl06 System.Web.UI.LiteralControl
    ctl07
```

The root node in the control tree is the page itself. The page has an ID of __Page. The page class contains all the other controls in its child controls collection.

The control tree also contains an instance of the HtmlForm class named form1. This control is the server-side form tag contained in the page. It contains all the other form controls—the DropDownList and Button controls—as child controls.

Notice that there are several LiteralControl controls interspersed between the other controls in the control tree. What are these controls?

Remember that everything in an ASP.NET page is converted into a .NET class, including any HTML or plain text content in a page. The LiteralControl class represents the HTML content in the page (including any carriage returns between tags).

NOTE

Normally, you refer to a control in a page by its ID. However, there are situations in which this is not possible. In those cases, you can use the FindControl() method of the Control class to retrieve a control with a particular ID. The FindControl() method is similar to the JavaScript getElementById() method.

Using Code-Behind Pages

The ASP.NET framework (and Visual Web Developer) enables you to create two different types of ASP.NET pages. You can create both single-file and two-file ASP.NET pages.

In a single-file ASP.NET page, a single file contains both the page code and page controls. The page code is contained in a <script runat="server"> tag.

As an alternative to a single-file ASP.NET page, you can create a two-file ASP.NET page. A two-file ASP.NET page is normally referred to as a *code-behind* page. In a code-behind page, the page code is contained in a separate file.

NOTE

Code-behind pages work in a different way in the ASP.NET 2.0 framework than they did in the ASP.NET 1.x framework. In ASP.NET 1.x, the two halves of a code-behind page were related by inheritance. In the ASP.NET 2.0 framework, the two halves of a code-behind page are related by a combination of partial classes and inheritance.

For example, Listing 13 and Listing 14 contain the two halves of a code-behind page.

VISUAL WEB DEVELOPER NOTE

When using Visual Web Developer, you create a code-behind page by selecting **Web Site**, **Add New Item**, selecting the **Web Form** item, and checking the Place Code in Separate File check box before adding the page.

Listing 13   FirstPageCodeBehind.aspx

```
<%@ Page Language="VB" AutoEventWireup="false"
CodeFile="FirstPageCodeBehind.aspx.vb" Inherits="FirstPageCodeBehind" %>
<!DOCTYPE html PUBLIC "-//W3C//DTD XHTML 1.0 Transitional//EN"
"http://www.w3.org/TR/xhtml1/DTD/xhtml1-transitional.dtd">
<html xmlns="http://www.w3.org/1999/xhtml" >
<head id="Head1" runat="server">
    <title>First Page Code-Behind</title>
</head>
<body>
    <form id="form1" runat="server">
    <div>

    <asp:Button
        id="Button1"
        Text="Click Here"
        Runat="server" />

    <br /><br />

    <asp:Label
        id="Label1"
        Runat="server" />

    </div>
    </form>
</body>
</html>
```

Listing 14   FirstPageCodeBehind.aspx.vb

```
Partial Class FirstPageCodeBehind
    Inherits System.Web.UI.Page


    Protected Sub Page_Load(ByVal sender As Object, ByVal e As System.EventArgs) _
    Handles Me.Load
        Label1.Text = "Click the Button"
    End Sub


    Protected Sub Button1_Click(ByVal sender As Object, ByVal e _
    As System.EventArgs) Handles Button1.Click
        Label1.Text = "Thanks!"
    End Sub


End Class
```

The page in Listing 13 is called the presentation page. It contains a `Button` control and a `Label` control. However, the page does not contain any code. All the code is contained in the code-behind file.

VISUAL WEB DEVELOPER NOTE

You can flip to the code-behind file for a page by right-clicking a page and selecting **View Code**.

The code-behind file in Listing 14 contains the `Page_Load()` and `Button1_Click()` handlers. The code-behind file in Listing 14 does not contain any controls.

Notice that the page in Listing 13 includes both a `CodeFile` and `Inherits` attribute in its `<%@ Page %>` directive. These attributes link the page to its code-behind file.

How Code-Behind Works: The Ugly Details

In the previous version of the ASP.NET framework (ASP.NET 1.x), two classes were generated by a code-behind page. One class corresponded to the presentation page and one class corresponded to the code-behind file. These classes were related to one another through class inheritance. The presentation page class inherited from the code-behind file class.

The problem with this method of associating presentation pages with their code-behind files was that it was very brittle. Inheritance is a one-way relationship. Anything that is true of the mother is true of the daughter, but not the other way around. Any control that you declared in the presentation page was required to be declared in the code-behind file. Furthermore, the control had to be declared with exactly the same ID. Otherwise, the inheritance relationship would be broken and events raised by a control could not be handled in the code-behind file.

In the beta version of ASP.NET 2.0, a completely different method of associating presentation pages with their code-behind files was used. This new method was far less brittle. Instead of relating the two halves of a code-behind page through inheritance, the two halves of a code-behind page were related through a new technology supported by the .NET 2.0 framework called partial classes.

Partial classes enable you to declare a class in more than one physical file. When the class gets compiled, one class is generated from all the partial classes. Any members of one partial class—including any private fields, methods, and properties—are accessible to any other partial classes of the same class. This makes sense because, at the end of the day, partial classes are combined to create one final class.

The advantage of using partial classes is that you don't need to worry about declaring a control in both the presentation page and code-behind file. Anything that you declare in the presentation page is automatically available in the code-behind file and anything you declare in the code-behind file is automatically available in the presentation page.

The beta version of the ASP.NET 2.0 framework used partial classes to relate a presentation page with its code-behind file. However, there were certain advanced features of the ASP.NET 1.x framework that were not compatible with using partial classes. To support these advanced features, a more complex method of associating presentation pages with code-behind files is used in the final release of the ASP.NET 2.0 framework.

NOTE

The ASP.NET 1.x framework enabled you to create a custom base Page class and inherit every ASP.NET page in an application from the custom Page class. Relating pages and code-behind files with partial classes conflicted with inheriting from a custom base Page class. In the final release of the ASP.NET 2.0 framework, you can once again create custom base Page classes.

The final release of the ASP.NET 2.0 framework uses a combination of inheritance and partial classes to relate presentation pages and code-behind files. The ASP.NET 2.0 framework generates three classes whenever you create a code-behind page.

The first two classes correspond to the presentation page. For example, when you create the FirstPageCodeBehind.aspx page, the following two classes are generated automatically in the Temporary ASP.NET Files folder:

```
Partial Public Class FirstPageCodeBehind

  Protected WithEvents Button1 As Global.System.Web.UI.WebControls.Button
  Protected WithEvents Label1 As Global.System.Web.UI.WebControls.Label
  ... additional class code ...


End Class

Public Class firstpagecodebehind_aspx
  Inherits FirstPageCodeBehind

  ... additional class code ...


End Class
```

A third class is generated that corresponds to the code-behind file. Corresponding to the FirstPageCodeBehind.aspx.vb file, the following class is generated:

```
Partial Class FirstPageCodeBehind
  Inherits System.Web.UI.Page


  Protected Sub Button1_Click(ByVal sender As Object, ByVal e As System.EventArgs) _
  Handles Button1.Click

    Label1.Text = "Thanks!"

  End Sub


End Class
```

The FirstPageCodeBehind_aspx class is executed when the FirstPageCodeBehind.aspx page is requested from a browser. This class inherits from the FirstPageCodeBehind class. The FirstPageCodeBehind class is a partial class. It gets generated twice: once by the presentation page and once by the code-behind file.

The final release of the ASP.NET 2.0 framework uses a combination of partial classes and inheritance to relate presentation pages and code-behind files. Because the page and code-behind classes are partial classes, unlike the previous version of ASP.NET, you no longer need to declare controls in both the presentation and code-behind page. Any control declared in the presentation page is accessible in the code-behind file automatically. Because the page class inherits from the code-behind class, the ASP.NET 2.0 framework continues to support advanced features of the ASP.NET 1.x framework, such as custom base Page classes.

Deciding Between Single-File and Code-Behind Pages

So, when should you use single-file ASP.NET pages and when should you use code-behind pages? This decision is a preference choice. There are intense arguments over this topic contained in blogs spread across the Internet.

I've heard it argued that code-behind pages are superior to single-file pages because code-behind pages enable you to more cleanly separate your user interface from your application logic. The problem with this argument is that the normal justification for separating your user interface from your application logic is code reuse. Building code-behind pages really doesn't promote code reuse. A better way to reuse application logic across multiple pages is to build separate component libraries.

My personal preference is to build ASP.NET applications using single-file ASP.NET pages because this approach requires managing fewer files. However, I've built many applications using the code-behind model (such as some of the ASP.NET Starter Kits) without suffering dire consequences.

NOTE

The previous version of Visual Studio .NET did not support building single-file ASP.NET pages. If you wanted to create single-file ASP.NET pages in the previous version of ASP.NET, you had to use an alternate development environment such as Web Matrix or Notepad.

Handling Page Events

Whenever you request an ASP.NET page, a particular set of events is raised in a particular sequence. This sequence of events is called the page execution lifecycle.

For example, we have already used the Page Load event in previous code samples in this introduction. You normally use the Page Load event to initialize the properties of controls contained in a page. However, the Page Load event is only one event supported by the Page class.

Here is the sequence of events that are raised whenever you request a page:

- PreInit
- Init
- InitComplete
- PreLoad
- Load

- LoadComplete
- PreRender
- PreRenderComplete
- SaveStateComplete
- Unload

Why so many events? Different things happen and different information is available at different stages in the page execution lifecycle.

For example, View State is not loaded until after the InitComplete event. Data posted to the server from a form control, such as a TextBox control, is also not available until after this event.

Ninety-nine percent of the time, you won't handle any of these events except for the Load and the PreRender events. The difference between these two events is that the Load event happens before any control events and the PreRender event happens after any control events.

The page in Listing 15 illustrates the difference between the Load and PreRender events. The page contains three event handlers: one for the Load event, one for the Button Click event, and one for the PreRender event. Each handler adds a message to a Label control (Figure 57).

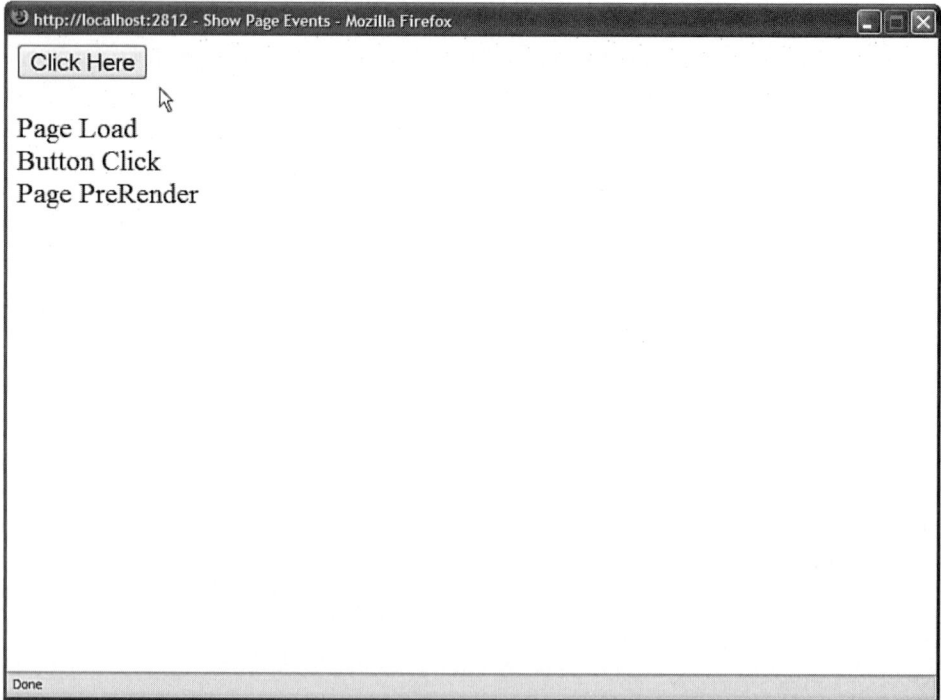

Figure 57   Viewing the sequence of page events.

Listing 15   ShowPageEvents.aspx

```
<%@ Page Language="VB" %>
<!DOCTYPE html PUBLIC "-//W3C//DTD XHTML 1.0 Transitional//EN"
    "http://www.w3.org/TR/xhtml1/DTD/xhtml1-transitional.dtd">
<script runat="server">

    Sub Page_Load()
        Label1.Text = "Page Load"
    End Sub


    Sub Button1_Click(ByVal sender As Object, ByVal e As EventArgs)
        Label1.Text &= "<br />Button Click"
    End Sub


    Sub Page_PreRender()
        Label1.Text &= "<br />Page PreRender"
    End Sub
</script>
<html xmlns="http://www.w3.org/1999/xhtml" >
<head id="Head1" runat="server">
    <title>Show Page Events</title>
</head>
<body>
    <form id="form1" runat="server">
    <div>

    <asp:Button
        id="Button1"
        Text="Click Here"
        OnClick="Button1_Click"
        Runat="server" />

    <br /><br />

    <asp:Label
        id="Label1"
        Runat="server" />

    </div>
    </form>
</body>
</html>
```

When you click the Button control, the Click event does not happen on the server until after the Load event and before the PreRender event.

The other thing you should notice about the page in Listing 15 is the way the event handlers are wired to the `Page` events. ASP.NET pages support a feature named `AutoEventWireUp`, which is enabled by default. If you name a subroutine `Page_Load()`, the subroutine automatically handles the `Page Load` event; if you name a subroutine `Page_PreRender()`, the subroutine automatically handles the `Page PreRender` event, and so on.

WARNING

`AutoEventWireUp` does not work for every page event. For example, it does not work for the `Page_InitComplete()` event.

Using the Page.IsPostBack Property

The `Page` class includes a property called the `IsPostBack` property, which you can use to detect whether the page has already been posted back to the server.

Because of View State, when you initialize a control property, you do not want to initialize the property every time a page loads. Because View State saves the state of control properties across page posts, you typically initialize a control property only once, when the page first loads.

In fact, many controls don't work correctly if you re-initialize the properties of the control with each page load. In these cases, you must use the `IsPostBack` property to detect whether the page has been posted.

The page in Listing 16 illustrates how you can use the `Page.IsPostBack` property when adding items to a `DropDownList` control.

Listing 16   ShowIsPostBack.aspx

```
<%@ Page Language="VB" %>
<!DOCTYPE html PUBLIC "-//W3C//DTD XHTML 1.0 Transitional//EN"
    "http://www.w3.org/TR/xhtml1/DTD/xhtml1-transitional.dtd">
<script runat="server">

    Sub Page_Load()
        if Not Page.IsPostBack Then
            ' Create collection of items
            Dim items As New ArrayList()
            items.Add("Apples")
            items.Add("Oranges")

            ' Bind to DropDownList
            DropDownList1.DataSource = items
            DropDownList1.DataBind()
        End If
    End Sub
```

```
    Sub Button1_Click(ByVal sender As Object, ByVal e As EventArgs)
        Label1.Text = DropDownList1.SelectedItem.Text
    End Sub
</script>
<html xmlns="http://www.w3.org/1999/xhtml" >
<head id="Head1" runat="server">
    <title>Show IsPostBack</title>
</head>
<body>
    <form id="form1" runat="server">
    <div>

    <asp:DropDownList
        id="DropDownList1"
        Runat="server" />

    <asp:Button
        id="Button1"
        Text="Select"
        OnClick="Button1_Click"
        Runat="server" />

    <br /><br />

    You selected:
    <asp:Label
        id="Label1"
        Runat="server" />

    </div>
    </form>
</body>
</html>
```

In Listing 16, the code in the Page_Load() event handler executes only once when the page first loads. When you post the page again, the IsPostBack property returns True and the code contained in the Page_Load() handler is skipped.

If you remove the IsPostBack check from the Page_Load() method, you get a strange result. The DropDownList always displays its first item as the selected item. Binding the DropDownList to a collection of items re-initializes the DropDownList control. Therefore, you want to bind the DropDownList control only once, when the page first loads.

Debugging and Tracing ASP.NET Pages

The sad fact of life is that, when building applications, you spend the majority of your development time debugging the application.

In this section, you learn how to get detailed error messages when developing ASP.NET pages. You also learn how you can display custom trace messages that you can use when debugging a page.

Debugging ASP.NET Pages

If you need to view detailed error messages when you execute a page, you need to enable debugging for either the page or your entire application. You can enable debugging for a page by adding a Debug="true" attribute to the <%@ Page %> directive. For example, the page in Listing 17 has debugging enabled.

Listing 17   ShowError.aspx

```
<%@ Page Language="VB" Debug="true" %>
<!DOCTYPE html PUBLIC "-//W3C//DTD XHTML 1.0 Transitional//EN"
 "http://www.w3.org/TR/xhtml1/DTD/xhtml1-transitional.dtd">
<script runat="server">

    Sub Page_Load()
        Dim Blow
        Label1.Text = Blow.Up()
    End Sub

</script>
<html xmlns="http://www.w3.org/1999/xhtml" >
<head id="Head1" runat="server">
    <title>Show Error</title>
</head>
<body>
    <form id="form1" runat="server">
    <div>

    <asp:Label
        id="Label1"
        Runat="server" />

    </div>
    </form>
</body>
    </html>
```

When you open the page in Listing 17 in your web browser, a detailed error message is displayed (see Figure 58).

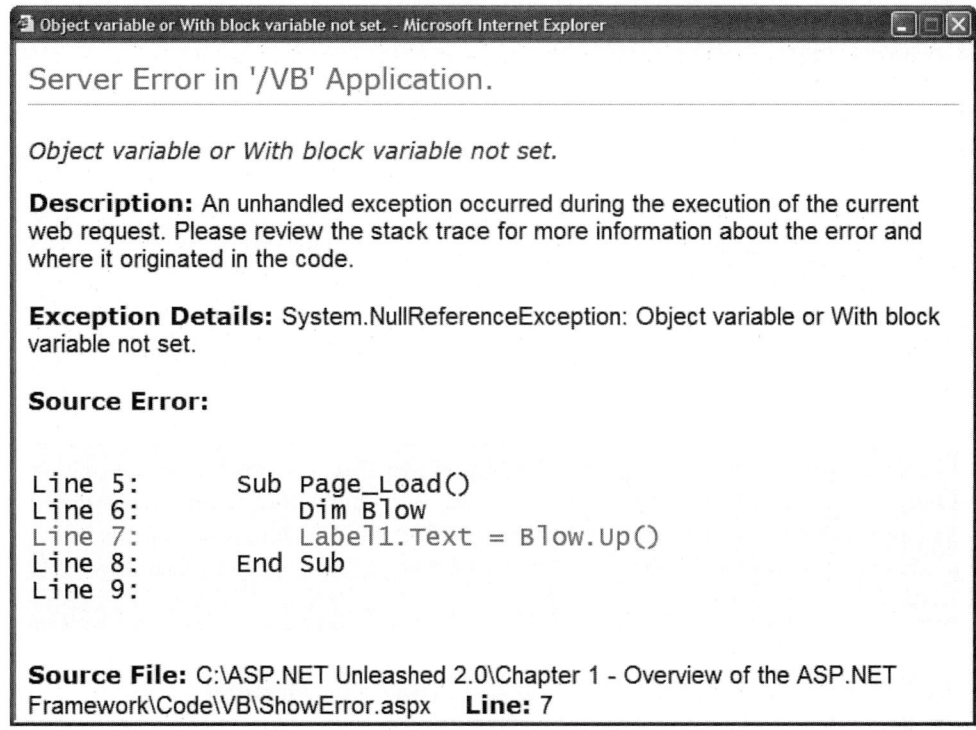

Figure 58   Viewing a detailed error message.

WARNING

Make sure that you disable debugging before placing your application into production. When an application is compiled in debug mode, the compiler can't make certain performance optimizations.

Rather than enable debugging for a single page, you can enable debugging for an entire application by adding the web configuration file in Listing 18 to your application.

Listing 18   Web.Config

```
<?xml version="1.0"?>
<configuration>
<system.web>
  <compilation debug="true" />
</system.web>
</configuration>
```

When debugging an ASP.NET application located on a remote web server, you need to disable custom errors. For security reasons, by default, the ASP.NET framework doesn't display error messages when you request a page from a remote machine. When custom errors are enabled, you don't see errors on a remote machine. The modified web configuration file in Listing 19 disables custom errors.

Listing 19   Web.Config

```xml
<?xml version="1.0"?>
<configuration>
<system.web>
  <compilation debug="true" />
  <customErrors mode="Off" />
</system.web>
</configuration>
```

Debugging Pages with Visual Web Developer

If you are using Visual Web Developer, you can display compilation error messages by performing a build on a page or an entire website. Select the menu option **Build**, **Build Page** or the menu option **Build**, **Build Web Site**. A list of compilation error messages and warnings appears in the Error List window (see Figure 59). You can double-click any of the errors to navigate directly to the code that caused the error.

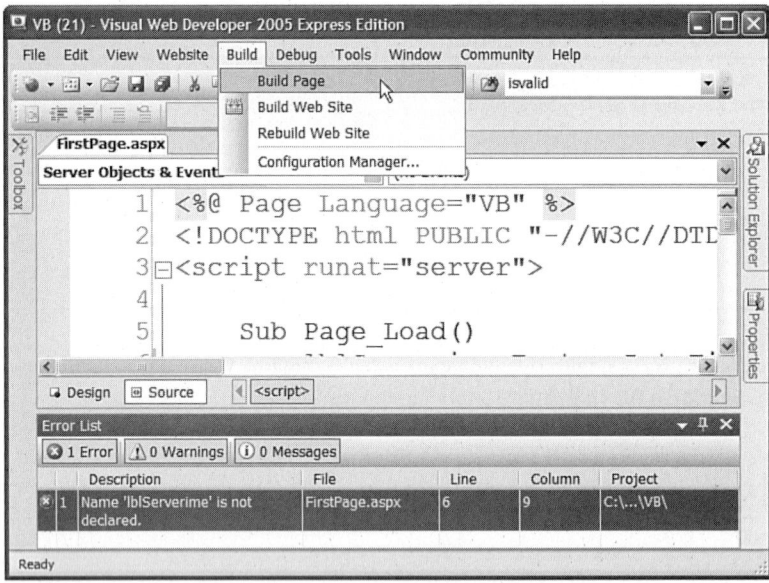

Figure 59   Performing a build in Visual Web Developer.

If you need to perform more advanced debugging, you can use the Visual Web Developer's debugger. The debugger enables you to set breakpoints and step line by line through your code.

You set a breakpoint by double-clicking the leftmost column in Source view. When you add a breakpoint, a red circle appears (see Figure 60).

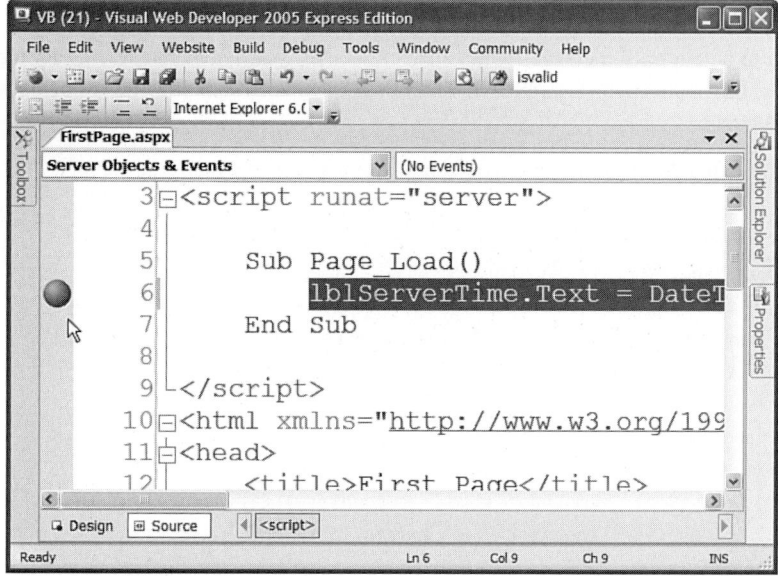

Figure 60   Setting a breakpoint.

After you set a breakpoint, run your application by selecting the menu option Debug, **Start Debugging**. Execution stops when the breakpoint is hit. At that point, you can hover your mouse over any variable or control property to view the current value of the variable or control property.

NOTE

You can designate one of the pages in your application as the start page. That way, whenever you run your application, the start page is executed regardless of the page that you have open. Set the start page by right-clicking a page in the Solution Explorer window and selecting the menu option **Set As Start Page**.

After you hit a breakpoint, you can continue execution by selecting **Step Into**, **Step Over**, or **Step Out** from the Debug menu or the toolbar. Here's an explanation of each of these options:

- **Step Into**—Executes the next line of code

- **Step Over**—Executes the next line of code without leaving the current method

- **Step Out**—Executes the next line of code and returns to the method that called the current method

When you are finished debugging a page, you can continue, stop, or restart your application by selecting a particular option from the Debug menu or the toolbar.

Tracing Page Execution

If you want to output trace messages while a page executes, you can enable tracing for a particular page or an entire application. The ASP.NET framework supports both page-level tracing and application-level tracing.

The page in Listing 20 illustrates how you can take advantage of page-level tracing.

Listing 20   PageTrace.aspx

```
<%@ Page Language="VB" Trace="true" %>
<!DOCTYPE html PUBLIC "-//W3C//DTD XHTML 1.0 Transitional//EN"
    "http://www.w3.org/TR/xhtml1/DTD/xhtml1-transitional.dtd">
<script runat="server">

    Sub Page_Load()
        For counter As Integer = 0 To 9
            ListBox1.Items.Add("item " & counter.ToString())
            Trace.Warn("counter=" & counter.ToString())
        Next
    End Sub

</script>
<html xmlns="http://www.w3.org/1999/xhtml" >
<head id="Head1" runat="server">
    <title>Page Trace</title>
</head>
<body>
    <form id="form1" runat="server">
    <div>

    <asp:ListBox
        id="ListBox1"
        Runat="server" />

    </div>
    </form>
</body>
</html>
```

Notice that the <%@ Page %> directive in Listing 20 includes a trace="true" attribute. This attribute enables tracing and causes a Trace Information section to be appended to the bottom of the page (see Figure 61).

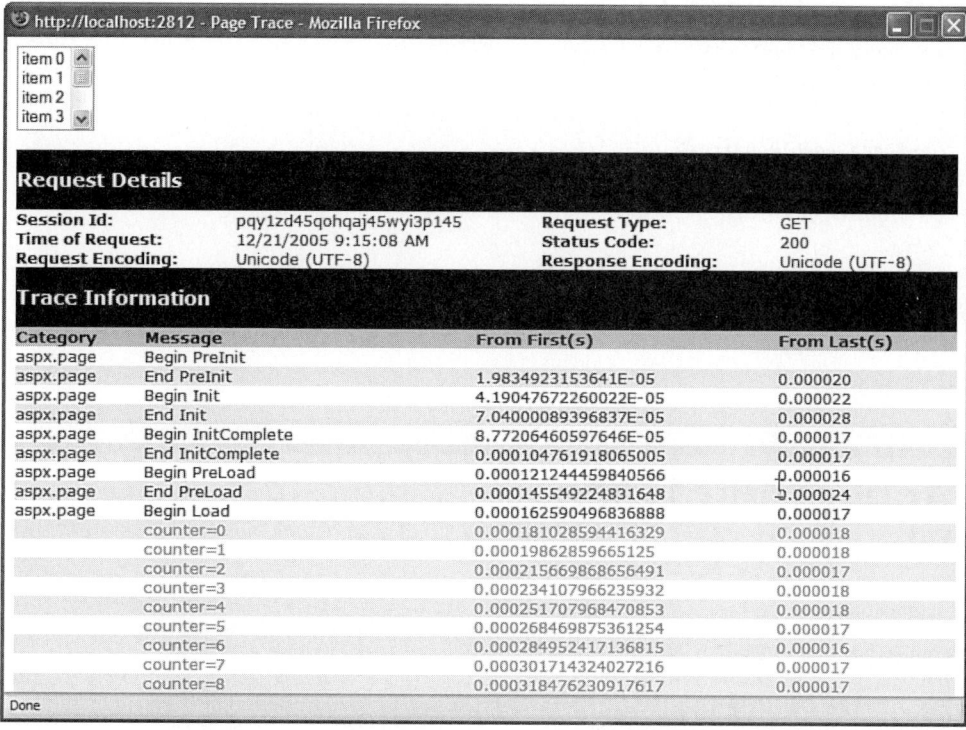

Figure 61   Viewing page trace information.

Notice, furthermore, that the Page_Load() handler uses the Trace.Warn() method to write messages to the Trace Information section. You can output any string to the Trace Information section that you please. In Listing 20, the current value of a variable named counter is displayed.

You'll want to take advantage of page tracing when you need to determine exactly what is happening when a page executes. You can call the Trace.Warn() method wherever you need in your code. Because the Trace Information section appears even when there is an error in your page, you can use tracing to diagnose the causes of any page errors.

One disadvantage of page tracing is that everyone in the world gets to see your trace information. You can get around this problem by taking advantage of application-level tracing. When application-level tracing is enabled, trace information appears only when you request a special page named Trace.axd.

To enable application-level tracing, you need to add the web configuration file in Listing 21 to your application.

Listing 21   Web.Config

```xml
<?xml version="1.0"?>
<configuration>
<system.web>
    <trace enabled="true" />
</system.web>
</configuration>
```

After you add the Web.Config file in Listing 21 to your application, you can request the Trace.axd page in your browser. The last 10 page requests made after application-level tracing is enabled are displayed (see Figure 62).

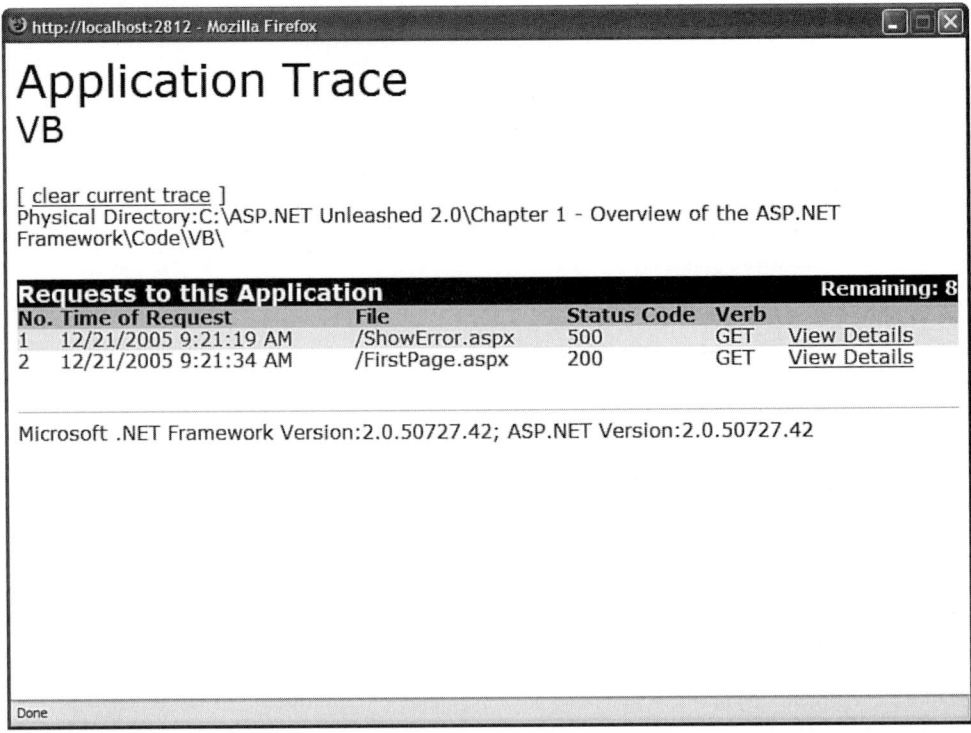

Figure 62   Viewing application trace information.

WARNING

By default, the Trace.axd page cannot be requested from a remote machine. If you need to access the Trace.axd page remotely, you need to add a localOnly="false" attribute to the trace element in the web configuration file.

If you click the View Details link next to any of the listed page requests, you can view all the trace messages outputted by the page. Messages written with the `Trace.Warn()` method are displayed by the Trace.axd page even when page-level tracing is disabled.

NOTE

You can use the new `writeToDiagnosticsTrace` attribute of the `trace` element to write all trace messages to the Output window of Visual Web Developer when you run an application. You can use the new `mostRecent` attribute to display the last 10 page requests rather than the 10 page requests after tracing was enabled.

Installing the ASP.NET Framework

The easiest way to install the ASP.NET framework is to install Visual Web Developer Express. You can download the latest version of Visual Web Developer Express from www.ASP.net, which is the official Microsoft ASP.NET website.

Installing Visual Web Developer Express also installs the following components:

- Microsoft .NET Framework version 2.0
- SQL Server Express

Visual Web Developer Express is compatible with the following operating systems:

- Windows 2000 Service Pack 4
- Windows XP Service Pack 2
- Windows Server 2003 Service Pack 1
- Windows x64 editions
- Windows Vista

I strongly recommend that you also download the .NET Framework SDK (Software Development Kit). The SDK includes additional documentation, sample code, and tools for building ASP.NET applications. You can download the SDK from the Microsoft MSDN website located at msdn.microsoft.com.

You can install Visual Web Developer Express on a computer that already has Visual Studio .NET 2003 installed. The two development environments can co-exist peacefully.

Furthermore, the same web server can serve both ASP.NET 1.1 pages and ASP.NET 2.0 pages. Each version of the .NET Framework is installed in the following folder:

C:\WINDOWS\Microsoft.NET\Framework

For example, on my computer, I have the following three versions of the .NET Framework installed (version 1.0, version 1.1, and version 2.0):

C:\WINDOWS\Microsoft.NET\Framework\v1.0.3705

C:\WINDOWS\Microsoft.NET\Framework\v1.1.4322

C:\WINDOWS\Microsoft.NET\Framework\v2.0.50727

Each folder includes a command-line tool named aspnet_regiis.exe. You can use this tool to associate a particular virtual directory on your machine with a particular version of the .NET Framework.

For example, executing the following command from a command prompt enables a particular version of ASP.NET for a virtual directory named MyApplication:

```
aspnet_regiis -s W3SVC/1/ROOT/MyApplication
```

By executing the aspnet_regiis.exe tool located in the different .NET Framework version folders, you can map a particular virtual directory to any version of the ASP.NET framework.

livelessons ▶

video instruction from technology experts

Trying to keep your skills up to date with the latest technology and advance your career?

Tired of expensive off-site training programs?

Wish you could learn from the best technologists in the industry?

LiveLessons: self-paced, personal video instruction from the world's leading technology experts

- INSTRUCTORS YOU TRUST
- CUTTING EDGE TOPICS
- CUSTOMIZED, SELF-PACED LEARNING
- LEARN BY DOING

The power of the world's leading experts at your fingertips!

To learn more about **LiveLessons** visit
www.mylivelessons.com

 Addison Wesley PRENTICE HALL  SAMS